GLOBAL GOVERNANCE
THE BATTLE OVER PLANETARY POWER

Kristin Dawkins

AN OPEN MEDIA BOOK

SEVEN STORIES PRESS
New York

In Canada: Hushion House, 36 Northline Road, Toronto, Ontario M4B 3E2

In the U.K.: Turnaround Publisher Services Ltd., Unit 3, Olympia Trading Estate, Coburg Road, Wood Green, London N22 6TZ

In Australia: Palgrave Macmillan, 627 Chapel Street, South Yarra, VIC 3141

Cover design: Greg Ruggiero
Cover image: Protesters carry an inflatable globe during an anti-war demonstration, February 15, 2003, in New York City. The rally coincided with peace demonstrations around the world. MARIO TAMA/GETTY IMAGES

ISBN 1-58322-580-3

Printed in Canada.

9 8 7 6 5 4 3 2 1

THANKS TO

Mr. Chakravarthi Raghavan, chief editor of the *South-North Development Monitor* (*SUNS*), who has spent more than four decades covering the challenge of just governance within the multilateral system;

and

IN LOVING MEMORY OF

Paul and Sheila Wellstone, and all those who have lost their lives while working for justice.

May 2003

CONTENTS

ACKNOWLEDGMENTS

There are experts far greater than I on the various topics I attempt to discuss in this little book. They will certainly notice that in stating matters for the purpose of providing a broad overview, I have simplified many things—hopefully not to the point of inaccuracy. Further to that, any and all feedback is welcome. Many thanks to Sophia Murphy and Andre Lambelet for their careful review and to Ria Julien for her superb edits. And a special thank-you to all of my friends across the planet from whom I have learned over the years about the complexity of the world and those who manage its human affairs.

STARTING AT HOME

In my neighborhood in St. Paul, Minnesota, there's a strong will among neighbors to decide our community's future for ourselves—what new developments or demolition will come next. Affordable housing, home ownership, problem properties, and crime are big issues here. We've campaigned for better schools and to make sure there are safe places for our kids to play, and we've worked to clean up the toxic rail yard next door.

This is St. Paul's East Side, traditionally a working-class area with a strong sense of identity. Europeans settled here at the turn of the twentieth century—Swedes, Irish, Italians, Norwegians, and Poles. Mexicans came during the early 1900s. All these immigrants arrived by rail and squatted along Phalen Creek in Swede Hollow before gradually moving up into the more established communities on the bluff lands of the Mississippi River. Here, virtually all of the businesses on the main street are family-owned and -operated. People know each other. They take care of each other. It feels like a small town.

But there is hardship here. The elimination of thousands of blue-collar jobs has disturbed this community's sense of security. We are now the second-poorest community of all St. Paul and have the highest crime statistics. The largest Native American community in St. Paul lives here too. People of color now make up the majority of this neighborhood. Many old-timers are moving away, and many new immigrants from Laos and Cambodia, Mexico, and Somalia have moved in. They all had reasons for leaving where they were and choosing to come here. Generally, people only move when they have to, or when they see hope for a better life somewhere else. In the nearest public grade school, some ninety percent of the kids move every year. The kind of transience evidenced in St. Paul, Minnesota, and, indeed, throughout most of the world, is proof positive that global conditions are far from okay.

Can we build an inclusive multicultural community on the East Side of St. Paul that is both financially healthy and socially happy? I think we can. In my view, it depends on sustaining and strengthening the democratic principles and organizations for which Minnesota is famous. Our democratic-farm-labor party, part of the national Democratic Party, has roots deep in the populist era of the farm and labor movements of the early twentieth century. Yet popular participation and commitment to populist economics in St. Paul, like everywhere else, have faded over the years.

Globalization has permeated St. Paul's East Side, just as it is permeating most communities on Earth. No matter the locale, people are reacting to the loss of control over their futures. In my neighborhood, the business association has not sought to attract corporate chain franchises; we are developing through investments in family-owned businesses. In my neighborhood, the development company is committed to generating wealth for the people who already live here, and it stands by the principle that we can do this better together—all of us, the current residents of the East Side. Recently, this community elected the first Hmong person to any state legislature in the United States, to the Minnesota Senate. And she is a Hmong woman—a refugee from Laos after the Vietnam War—named Mee Moua. Senator Moua's victory demonstrates that community strength and political power can rise quite literally from the ashes of displacement and social destruction—and a shared vision for the future can be defined across our cultural differences.

Still, if transnational corporate interests are allowed to continue their raid on human resources, natural resources, and financial resources in every country on Earth, the future appears grim.

If, on the other hand, we can develop the capacity to control our immediate neighborhoods, the knowledge and strength to achieve accountability from our municipal and regional governments, the collective wisdom and power to structure a more democratic formation of national government, and the friendships and global solidarity to create an international system of just governance—why, there just may be a future we need not fear for our children.

This is our goal.

WHO'S IN CHARGE?

Who's in charge of this planet, anyway?

Watching the news, attending civic meetings, noting the state of schools and hospitals in decay, or reading the ticker tape of the ever-moving stock markets, you, like me, may feel confounded. It's hard to know who—if anyone—is pulling the strings as events whiz by at breakneck pace.

Some would say it's the United States of America itself—the world's current superpower. U.S. military, economic, and political power have for many years been driving a host of changes on this planet, including dramatic shifts in international alliances and institutions. Historically, the United States has played a major role in creating the multilateral system, while nowadays it is more inclined to brazenly act on its own.

Some say it's the Group of Eight, often referred to as the G-8: the leaders of the eight richest countries in the world who get together every six months or so and think about coordinating their economic plans. But lately, the economy has been so screwy, that it seems they don't know how to fix it. And with divisions in their ranks over the war on Iraq, this group of global leaders may be sidelined for the time being.

Many observers would suggest a global power shift is emerging, with the European Union (EU) very deliberately forging an economic and political federation to counter U.S. hegemony. In part, the Bush administration's unilateral warmongering may be just as deliberately intending to disrupt such European unity. China and India, too, along with other Third World allies, have been accumulating political, economic, and military clout with which to challenge U.S. power. And some predict a new era of Latin American cooperation, marked by popular labor-friendly reformist governments in Brazil, Venezuela, Ecuador, and potentially Bolivia consolidating their interests and wealth.

Plenty of analysts might advise us to "Follow the money!" to get to the bottom of this, pointing to the central bankers of the U.S., German, and Japanese governments, whose dollars and Euros and yen are considered the only precious currencies in the world. A nation's economy supposedly benefits from gaining these "hard currencies," as they are called, through exports, because they, more than other currencies, may be readily reinvested in the global economy.

Quite possibly, it's Citigroup and a handful of other private banking corporations whose executives sit in powerful positions within the G-8 governments, and whose computers charge rent as all data entriescross their screens. So far, they've managed to consolidate their financial empire into ever-greater pyramid schemes, but these are notoriously unsustainable without constantly issuing new credit. And sooner or later, credit bubbles tend to burst.

Lots of people would indicate it's the Fortune 500 companies, which have been merging and acquiring each other and political power such that they dominate the international marketplace and financial flows worldwide. When the transnational conglomerates can't bargain or buy their way past government regulations, they use their influence to deploy international economic organizations—particularly the World Trade Organization (WTO), World Bank, and International Monetary Fund (IMF)—as agencies for commercial promotion.

Some say that the WTO controls the global economy on behalf of the corporations. Founded in 1994, the WTO inherited the trade rules of the General Agreement on Tariffs and Trade (GATT) and its mandate to encourage commerce by lowering tariffs—the duties charged at the border on imports—and limiting how governments regulate food safety and other "nontariff barriers" to trade. The WTO added a bunch of new rules, too, freeing up the trading companies to do more international business with less interference from national governments.

Others might add that the World Bank and IMF support this private business agenda by lending funds contributed by the taxpayers of the industrialized countries to subsidize commercial enterprise. The World Bank finances the building of dams and harbors and roads needed to extract the natural resources of developing countries. Once extracted, these resources are sold to the mining, timber, shipping, and financial sectors that are increasingly made up of global companies. The IMF makes short-term loans to cover governments' cash flow problems. These loans are usually offered on the condition that the troubled government invests in export development instead of education, health, and human development, so as to ensure cash will flow in to pay off the loan. As a result, the business climate may improve—ripening the cherry for picking by foreign corporations—but local communities are left with the bill while the World Bank and IMF take control of their government's purse strings, seemingly forever.

Very few think the United Nations (UN) runs the world, although it demonstrated remarkable resistance in the Security Council to U.S. militancy against Iraq. Peace and human rights, food security, world health, child welfare, labor law, scientific and cultural and educational development, environmental protection, and so forth— all these are protected by international law as part of the UN's mandate. But the UN serves largely a moral force, because, alas, these global social agreements tend to be violated, especially by the United States. Put simply, the UN lacks enforcement capacity. Perhaps more important, it lacks the financial capability to invest and create incentives directed toward these and other goals for a more equitable future.

Many believe it's still national governments that make international decisions. While individual nation-states do have a voice and voting power in the existing framework of global governance, it's no secret that the World Bank and IMF have voting schemes weighted according to the financial contributions of the participating governments—so the poorer nations have virtually no say at all! And even though the WTO and all the UN treaties are set up according to a one nation–one vote scheme—except that many European nations now vote together as the EU—a few states with bigger economies tend to bully the others. Another glaring shortcoming is that indigenous peoples' governments are excluded from the definition of nation-states under the current multilateral system.

Whoever is running this planet, more and more people seem to agree that the rulers are not doing a very good job. The harsh reality faced by billions of people on this planet is one of dire poverty, and the past decade of modern globalization has intensified, not rectified, the inequities. During this time, the number of billionaires nearly tripled as the gap between the income of top corporate executives and average workers grew by a factor of ten—from 42:1 to 419:1. The miseries of war, infant mortality, childhood labor, inadequate food and water, poor sanitation, inadequate health care, and political oppression are increasingly the lot of most people on Earth.

Everywhere we turn, there is instability, insecurity, and uncertainty. Even middle-class Americans feel vulnerable and wonder what it will take to regain control over their lives, families, and communities. The September 11 attacks on New York City and Washington left the entire world searching to understand the "roots of violence," shredding capitalist complacency after the fall of the Berlin Wall. Organized groups frustrated with real and perceived injustices, inequities, and discrimination are lashing out against other citizens—with al-Qaeda at one extreme and the Bush administration at another. As a new government formed in Afghanistan, tribal groups there struggled to find an acceptable balance of power, and yet the United States continues to meddle in their internal affairs and enlarge the scope of its campaign against terrorism and the "axis of evil." Inside the United States, the new USA PATRIOT Act rescinds a host of basic civil rights and enables the government to label "antiglobalization" organizations as "terrorist." And when President Bush finally attacked Iraq without UN support, the violence not only led to the killing and maiming of thousands of civilians and soldiers, it castrated the basic authority and relevance of the UN's multilateral mission.

At the same time, there is a growing debate among human rights groups and constitutional scholars about these matters, a new interest in Islamic culture, strengthened support for peace in the Middle East, greater clarity about the oil trade, and an increased understanding of U.S. responsibility to the international community. Peace rallies have been organized on every continent against the war on Iraq, and the Internet-assisted global campaign to wage peace has even prompted one of the original founders of the UN, Robert Muller, to exclaim with a tear in his eye: "Never before in the history of the world has there been a global, visible, public, viable, open dialogue and conversation about the very legitimacy of war."

All over the world, there is a much greater awareness of our collective interdependence, as well as the mechanics of global governance. In response to the expanding war on terror, public education campaigns regarding the WTO, IMF, World Bank, and UN are scrutinizing not just the economic roots of violence, but also the elements of democratic reconstruction and the differences between unilateral and multilateral peacekeeping and warmongering. Everyone is asking, How can we go about altering the balance of power on Earth justly?

There are at least three very distinct responses to this question. One, a traditional revolutionary response, asserts that those who are raking in billions of dollars from the unjust system will continue to be unwilling to improve their habits without being forced to through insurgency and direct confrontation. A second response pursues evolutionary adaptation, asserting that a series of modest reforms add up to real change. A third response asserts that a major nonviolent political shift is possible by coordinating well-organized movements in every country that would unite to abolish the existing institutions and re-create a decentralized system of democratic governance spanning the planet. Large segments of civil society can be found arguing for each of these views.

As the twenty-first century unfolds, we are likely to see more violence as well as political upheaval and incremental reform—and hopefully a rather different world than the one we now know. We can guess that it will turn out to be less than ideal, but it seems destined to be more responsive to the public. Together, the diverse strands of global civil society tend to agree that we must strive to bring about a more just and democratic approach to governance at every level, global to local, but perhaps most of all at the national level.

This is our project.

Part I

THE INTERNATIONAL INSTITUTIONS

Back in July 1944, a group of economists from forty-four countries convened in the small town of Bretton Woods, New Hampshire. Reeling from the stock market crash of 1929, the Great Depression of the thirties, and World War II, these planners designed the framework for today's international economic institutions. They wrote up the founding documents of the IMF and the World Bank and made plans to set up a trade organization. Four years later, they met again in Havana, Cuba, to sign doc- *1948* uments creating what they called the International Trade Organization (ITO), a body to function alongside the IMF and World Bank. (The ITO itself never materialized, but its stepchild, the GATT. eventually became today's WTO.)

During this postwar era, another group of diplomats set up the UN after an intensive process of citizen participation in hopes of finding political balance among the world's great powers of the time. Today, the UN, World Bank, IMF, and WTO dominate international policy making and exercise increasing control over national and local governments around the world.

23

In large part, the Bretton Woods meeting of 1944 was a series of debates between U.S. Treasury official Harry Dexter White and Great Britain's treasury representative, Lord John Maynard Keynes. White chaired the work on the IMF and Keynes chaired the work on the World Bank. There were many complex matters to resolve, of course, but their biggest disagreement seemed to be over national sovereignty. Basically, on behalf of the United States, Harry White was not prepared to give up one shred of U.S. autonomy to an international institution, while Lord Keynes favored depoliticizing the intergovernmental dynamic by creating universal rules governing all participating countries.

The World Bank, officially called the International Bank for Reconstruction and Development, was designed to fill the gap in private-lending markets for higher-risk projects in countries needing investment capital. White's proposals for the bank emphasized low-cost, long-term loans to rebuild productive capacity in the bombed-out ruins of Europe, while Lord Keynes spoke of the need to provide development assistance elsewhere in the world, including the European colonies and other poorer countries. In the end, an amendment offered by Mexico was adopted that recognized the immediate need for reconstruction in Europe, but which called for "equitable consideration to projects for development and projects for reconstruction alike."

The IMF was designed to stabilize the value of money,

based on the principle of balancing supply and demand. It would use short-term loans and a special type of credit named special drawing rights (SDRs) to prevent huge fluctuations in currency exchange rates. At the time, governments exercised regulatory control over capital and held deficits and surpluses in multiple currencies in their central banks. Keynes believed that a new global unit of currency would make it easier for countries to exchange the different national currencies, clearing up deficits and balancing the global money supply. Keynes also believed that IMF members should be "entitled" to buy each other's currencies or SDRs whenever they wanted—a genuine

free market. White, to the contrary, preferred that the IMF assist countries with their balance-of-payments problems using existing currencies, particularly the dollar, and argued assistance should be offered only when countries could *prove* a genuine need.

In the end, Keynes won that round 16-1, and the term "entitled" remains in the official IMF Articles of Agreement. However, White won the debate with the most enduring impact, pertaining to how these institutions are governed. Keynes wanted to employ a staff of professional, independent, international civil servants, but White insisted that they be managed by politically appointed executive directors operating full-time—and White won out. Arguably, directors representing their national governments might be a more democratic approach, but Keynes was wary of superpower dominance. And it turns out he was right.

To this day, the United States holds unquestionable dominance in both the IMF and World Bank. The dollar became the official currency, and the headquarters of both the IMF and World Bank were set up in Washington, D.C. Within five years, the IMF executive board set a ceiling on fund entitlements and started requiring consultations before their use. In 1952, they adopted the principle of "conditionalities," putting the burden of proof on recipients of IMF funds to show "whether the policies the member will pursue will be adequate to overcome the problem." This erosion of the entitlement concept paved the way for the injustices that now expose these institutions to such harsh criticism.

In 1969, the IMF board finally created a watered-down version of Keynes's proposal for a centralized currency-reserve system. SDRs are now issued from time to time and allocated among IMF members according to a quota system. Their value is determined as an average of the value of other hard currencies. They can be used as a means of payment or exchange among IMF members, and as a unit of account and payment for the IMF and other development banks.

At both the IMF and World Bank, each nation appoints a governor, usually a high-level minister, who exercises authority at an annual meeting. However, the governors delegate their authority for day-to-day management to a board of twenty-four executive directors. Voting power is distributed among these executive directors according to each government's financial contributions to the institutions.

The United States currently wields 17.5 percent of the total IMF voting power. Along with Germany's and Japan's roughly 6 percent each, the United Kingdom's and France's 5 percent each, Italy's 3.3 percent, Canada's 3 percent, the Netherlands' 2.4 percent, Belgium's 2.2 percent, Switzerland's 1.6 percent, and Sweden's 1.1 percent, the industrialized countries easily dominate with a majority vote. The developing countries, which become indebted by the expense of big projects such as dams and harbors and highways, have virtually no votes in the decision-making process. China, for example, has just 3 percent of the total, India and Brazil have less than 2 percent each, Bangladesh has 0.2 percent, while Somalia, Mongolia, and a host of other small economies each have just 0.02 percent of the voting power.

The percentages of voting power are slightly different for the World Bank, which nowadays consists of five different institutions collectively called the World Bank Group. To join the present-day International Bank for Reconstruction and Development (IBRD), a country must already be a member of the IMF. Membership in the other four institutions in the World Bank Group—the International Development Association (IDA), the International Finance Corporation (IFC), the Multilateral International Guarantee Agency (MIGA), and the International Center for the Settlement of Investment Disputes (ICSID)—requires membership in the IBRD. Basically, the IBRD and IDA lend money for public-sector projects, while the IFC and MIGA lend money to support private-sector projects. Each of the four has its own

document that sets out decision-making proce-
ne voting shares for each institution differ
ot all countries belong to every institution; but
titution, the total vote is divided up according
to each member country's quota in the IMF.

Typically, a country seeking IMF or World Bank support opens its books to a visiting team of IMF and World
Bank staff who then negotiate the terms for a new financing package. But in response to the deepening debt crisis
of the 1980s, these teams began to impose very strict conditionalities on the debtor countries—requiring immediate "structural adjustment" of their money supply, interest rates, and currency value with strict quantitative targets for reducing inflation. They demanded "austerity" in
the national budget, privatization of public companies,
and deregulation of trade and financial and capital markets. The upshot was to get governments out of the business of managing their national economies.

A decade of riots, economic crises, and the utter economic collapse of a number of countries—among them
Thailand, Russia, and Argentina—followed. By the late
1990s, this formula, dubbed the Washington Consensus,
was severely criticized for its negative impacts on many
poor countries. Certainly, squeezing ever more money
out of a country to pay off debt will never generate
resources for development. Another ultimately unsustainable way to repay loans is to intensify the conversion
of natural resources to cash: mining, timber, and fishing
all make great exports, but when they're gone, they're
gone. Yet the IMF and World Bank have consistently

advised governments to dig deeper mines
forests; and subsidize drift nets and t
farms, chemical fertilizers, and plantati
regardless of the impact on local com
though these extractive industries alre
capacity of the Earth to replenish itself

The disposal of hazardous wastes and
nants is certainly not a sustainable development strategy,
either, although it may generate economic activity.
Indeed, Lawrence Summers, who served a term as
President Clinton's secretary of the treasury, wrote in an
internal memo during his tenure as chief economist at
the World Bank, "I think the economic logic behind
dumping a load of toxic waste in the lowest wage country is impeccable.... I've always thought that underpopu-
lated countries in Africa are vastly under-polluted; their
air quality is probably vastly inefficiently low compared
to Los Angeles or Mexico City." The ensuing uproar led
the World Bank to issue a clarifying statement but, ironic or not, the Summers memo records the actual effect of
the World Bank's loan portfolio.

Similarly destructive of the society as a whole is the
constant movement of resources from the public to the
private sector. In 1993, the World Bank declared water an
"economic good" and began stressing market-based
approaches to water delivery. Nowadays the World Bank
and IMF subsidize corporations to install pipes and
meters rather than subsidizing consumption for the poor,
and condition their loans on the privatization of community water systems. A review of IMF loans in 2000 found

water privatization and higher prices for water services were requirements in twelve out of forty countries,
most of these in Africa. In 2001 in KwaZulu-Natal, South
Africa, water supplies were cut off for those too poor to
pay, resulting in an outbreak of cholera that killed at
least thirty-two people.

In response to intense public pressure, the governors
of the World Bank and IMF in 1996 created the Heavily
Indebted Poor Countries (HIPC) initiative for countries
whose debt burden was considered "unsustainable" and
unresolvable by existing debt relief programs. These
countries, mostly African, would be required to demon-
strate a good track record in implementing World
Bank–IMF adjustment programs. Qualifying countries
were expected to include their national civil society and
private sector in designing an economic strategy to benefit the poor.

In 1999, the governors decided to "enhance" HIPC and
require the preparation and implementation of detailed
Poverty Reduction Strategy Papers (PRSPs) as a condition
for the debt forgiveness and special loans available to
these impoverished countries. Given the demands of a
full-fledged PRSP, they decided to establish a less rigorous Interim PRSP, a kind of "PRSP lite" enabling the
poorest countries to qualify for interim assistance more
readily. Over time, HIPC countries performing well
under both the regular World Bank–IMF programs and
the national PRSP program could get up to a 90 percent
reduction in the present value of the debt owed to other
countries' national and commercial banks. At the same

time, the World Bank and IMF would also chip in with reductions in the debt owed them. In 2001, the enhanced HIPC Initiative freed thirty-four countries from over $50 billion in payments, at a total cost to the lenders of some $30 billion in net present-value terms, about half of which was provided by bilateral creditors and half by multilateral lenders.

But the total Third World debt burden is some $2.5 trillion! And that figure is up 34 percent since 1992. Critics point out that the HIPC goal of reducing debt to "sustainable" levels merely perpetuates the drain of resources from the African continent. The formula for calculating so-called sustainable payment levels is based on a country's export revenues—while the whole package is tied to the usual Washington Consensus conditions. When Ghana decided to accept HIPC conditions in exchange for HIPC debt relief, the public reaction was so negative that, according to the *Ghanian Chronicle* newspaper, "[I]nferior goods on the market are called HIPC; poor people are laughed at as having been stricken by HIPC and even people shirking their parental responsibilities try to justify it with the excuse that they are heavily indebted poor parents."

Joseph Stiglitz, the World Bank's chief economist from 1997 to 2000 and a critic of the Washington Consensus, blamed structural adjustment, austerity, and "market fundamentalism" for the financial crisis in Thailand that spread throughout East Asia. He then resigned—although some say he was kicked out. In 2001, with a Nobel Prize for economics in hand, Stiglitz called the whole approach "bad economics and bad politics." As it turns out, the staffs of the IMF and World Bank have been unable to tweak economies precisely enough; by definition, market fundamentalism simply can't meet the IMF and World Bank's ostensible goals of stabilizing economies, alleviating poverty, and supporting development. Some degree of government intervention is necessary.

Civil society campaigns have targeted the World Bank's and IMF's skewed investment policies and structural adjustment programs for decades. Human rights activists and environmentalists have stopped numerous big dam projects, although more than five hundred have been built in ninety-two countries, displacing some 10 million people from their homes. And some of the biggest—including the Three Gorges Dam under way in China and India's extensive Narmada and Sardar Sarovar projects—are still scheduled for completion. Gradually, however, these institutions have come to accept the need for social and environmental assessments of their projects, and are adopting more transparent procedures for planning and review. Many activists have welcomed the World Bank's attempts to accommodate their concerns, while remaining highly critical of the limited results.

Fifty years after helping to found the IMF and World Bank, Victor Urquidi, the Mexican delegate in Bretton Woods who in 1944 had successfully proposed the amendment calling for "equitable consideration to projects for development and projects for reconstruction alike," wrote a retrospective article about these institutions. Here's how he summed it up in 1994:

"Considerations about general development issues—the role of, say, electric power development in triggering other domestic or foreign investments and raising productivity, employment, and real wages—were not seen by the prevailing 'bankers' mentality as particularly interesting."

Yes, the record is clear. While they may have been founded with honorable intentions, the World Bank and IMF were hijacked along the way by corporate interests who perceive every investment as an opportunity to maximize their own profit, with little or no regard for the human dimension and social development.

THE WTO

Following the lead of the Bretton Woods planners, the drafters of the 1948 Havana Charter for ITO were very specific about protecting labor rights, ensuring employment and a rising standard of living, restricting monopoly power, stabilizing commodity prices, and setting out provisions that would help ensure "fair trade." If the whole ITO had been adopted, the world may have become a different place than it now is. Unfortunately, the Truman administration rejected the ITO package, leading to the adoption of only one of the elements of the proposed organization: the trade-promoting commercial rules of the General Agreement on Tariffs and Trade—the infamous GATT—which in 1994 formed the basis of the WTO.

Originally, the GATT was a hodgepodge of contracts between major trading partners. Decision making was based on bilateral agreements. For thousands of products—whether beef or leather goods, silk or cotton T-shirts, Fords or Toyotas, tractors or machine parts, agricultural pesticides or commodity grains—the major trading partners would negotiate with one another until settling on tariff reductions that would, like a tax reduction, stimulate more economic exchange. Then, once the major trading partners agreed to specific tariffs, they would be obliged under GATT law to apply the same deals to all their other trading partners—stimulating even more international economic activity.

That was Article I of the GATT rules, entirely adopted by the WTO in 1994. "Most Favored Nation" status means every government participating in the WTO must give all exporters from every other WTO member country equal tariff treatment—that is, the same treatment they would give to their favorite trading partner. So, for example, even if you prefer trading with Argentina instead of China for various geopolitical reasons, once China is a member of the trading club, Chinese corporations get the same access to your market as the Argentines. Supposedly, this ensures that the most efficient producers of each product get access to every market, maximizing productivity worldwide—the famous theory of "comparative advantage." But tremendous economies of scale and displacement result: Welcome, China! Good-bye, Hungary!

Article III of the GATT, also entirely adopted by the WTO, requires that governments treat foreign companies just as they do domestically based companies, even in cases where a government may prefer to procure goods and services from national companies to build up certain sectors of the economy, or even to support local economic development strategies. This "National Treatment" provision similarly ensures market access for the supposedly most efficient firms. So the United States has to allow Chinese traders into our markets (well, we already do), and China has to let U.S. corporations compete over there. Now just guess which ones will take over!

Although some exceptions were negotiated, these two provisions form the core of trade policy theory: "nondiscrimination" amongst countries and companies—so the competition of the so-called free market will bring the best products at the lowest prices to consumers. But by-the-book "free trade"—where all parties to a transaction have equal access to resources, information, technology, and markets—is simply a mythical ideal. Just think, there are more telephone connections in Manhattan than in all of sub-Saharan Africa! So does the ideal of nondiscrimination best advance by treating a company in Chad the same as one based in Manhattan? Or is this ideal best met by first building up Chad's telecommunications sector—not to mention health, education, and other basic services—before exposing Chad's economy to Most Favored Nation status, National Treatment, and the rest of the "free trade" panoply of deregulation?

In practice, contemporary trade deals have freed up transnational corporations to avoid national regulation and taxes, manipulate prices, absorb smaller-scale firms, and exploit workers as they wish. And competitive advantages only partly derive from genuine efficiency; with better capitalization, global conglomerates easily outcompete even the most efficient small or medium-sized enterprise. The complex structure of transnational corporations—with subsidiaries in a number of countries—enables them to take strategic advantage of each country's economic, social, and political characteristics. Countries with abundant natural resources are mined for raw materials; those with depressed wages get jobs in manufacturing; those with weak environmental standards become toxic wastelands. Finally, the structure of taxes, subsidies, and other political factors dramatically alter the economics of foreign direct investment from country to country. Cargill and other giant grain exporters, for example, benefit from an array of U.S. "export credits" that float taxpayer dollars to lower their shipping and marketing costs overseas.

In the 1970s, GATT negotiators went beyond tariffs, making "nontariff barriers" such as stringent environmental and food safety restrictions illegal unless a country can *prove* they are "scientific" and "necessary." Then the WTO agreements of 1994 went beyond trade policy altogether, adding "trade-related" issues like patents and investment finance to its scope.

In addition, the 1994 deal eliminated the nation-to-nation contractual nature of GATT negotiations, instead forming the WTO as an institution—basically, a type of club whose "members" must follow all of the club's rules. On paper, the WTO prefers consensus decision making but calls for majority voting when necessary. In practice, however, negotiations are organized strategically by the more economically powerful countries, which gang up on dissenters—usually the Third World. This is probably the chief reason the Seattle Ministerial meeting of 1999 failed: developing countries got sick and tired of being left out of the so-called Green Room, where the power brokers made their advance deals. Unfortunately, Green Room tactics have continued as Third World government negotiators are overwhelmed by the array of lawyers representing the United States, Europe, and other G-8 powers in the multiple negotiations that make up the WTO's ongoing agenda.

Furthermore, the WTO has not only legislative but also judicial powers: when one country complains that another has violated an existing rule, a dispute settlement panel deliberates in secret and renders an opinion. The loser can file an appeal, but the WTO Appellate Body's decision is final (unless all WTO members, including the plaintiffs and defendants, reject its decision—a quite unlikely occurrence). Losers have to change their practices, laws, or administrative procedures or face economic "retaliation" in the form of trade sanctions.

For example, on behalf of U.S. cattle growers who are losing some $200 million in beef sales to Europe every year, the U.S. trade representative declared the EU's ban on artificial growth hormones in beef an illegal trade barrier. After several years of disputing the case, the WTO Appellate Panel ruled that this European regulation had not passed the WTO test of being based on a "scientific" risk assessment, particularly because the EU had tested the impacts of the hormones directly on people (finding problems!) instead of testing the impacts of eating hormone-laden beef. The EU decided they'd rather pay the penalty—tariffs that basically doubled the price of hundreds of products exported to the United States, making them so expensive that the European exporting companies lost about $200 million in sales per year (equivalent to the value of lost beef sales)—than eat artificial growth hormones. By the way, the EU had offered to import $200 million of organic beef instead, but this of course did nothing to satisfy the mainstream cattle industry.

This system really only works between governments that can afford to battle each other economically. The United States and Europe can afford to go back and forth in their trade war—with the Europeans winning their complaint that U.S. export credits to subsidize the overseas operations of Boeing and Microsoft and thousands of other corporations are unfair to European companies, and the United States winning on beef and bananas. In the banana case, the European system of importing a higher quota of bananas from small independent producers in its former colonies was judged to be unfair discrimination against the Chiquita and Dole corporations. The current battle in this transcontinental trade war is over whether or not the Europeans' preference for non–genetically engineered foods and seeds is "scientific" and "necessary."

Imagine Mozambique, the poorest country in Africa, losing export revenues to defend a policy protecting local farmers! Nicaragua once won a GATT dispute against the United States, claiming discriminatory administration of sugar import quotas. This was during the Sandinista government, and the Reagan administration refused to comply with the GATT panel ruling, instead imposing a complete embargo on all trade with Nicaragua. The GATT panel took a look at the embargo and decided not to oppose it, since the only available trade remedy would have allowed Nicaragua to suspend trade with the United States—a useless remedy under the embargo!

At least under the GATT small countries as well as large ones had effective veto power over decisions to enforce sanctions. But, under the WTO, the Appellate Body's decisions are final. And to think, most less-developed countries can't begin to afford the legal costs of engaging in a WTO dispute, whether as plaintiff or defense.

Other innovations of the WTO enshrine "relevant international standards" with authority over national regulations. An obscure UN agency known as Codex Alimentarius (Latin for "food code") used to give good, sound technical advice about protecting food safety; now, with WTO-given authority, it's become a major political force dominated by transnational food manufacturers. The even more obscure International Standardization Organization (ISO) sets technical recommendations for internationally traded products, standardizing the size of the screw threads in lightbulbs, for example. But now the ISO is setting its sights on creating forestry and water standards—under the influence of giant timber and water corporations and with WTO authority backed by trade sanctions.

When corporate interests inside ISO and Codex turn their attention to the privatization of water treatment facilities or declare genetically engineered foods to be "substantially equivalent" to non–genetically engineered foods, the public interest suffers—especially when the WTO requires most of the world to adopt these standards. The argument here isn't one of whether international standards are appropriate, but one of democracy and justice: Who is making these decisions? Who benefits? Whose standards?

It is probably not an oversight that in 1994 the WTO negotiators neglected to list the International Labor Organization (ILO) as one of the "relevant international organizations" whose standards are given authority over WTO members' national laws. Its many conventions— protecting the rights of workers to organize, to bargain collectively, to strike and to otherwise defend their interests relative to their employers—are just not consistent with the corporate agenda. The ILO even has a convention defending the rights of indigenous peoples to their economic self-reliance, lands, and resources. Similarly, the WTO negotiators neglected to reference existing multilateral environmental agreements negotiated under UN auspices, which also contain standards protecting the rights of indigenous peoples and local communities, and are otherwise contrary to the corporate model of exploitative development.

Whether the WTO ever takes upon itself the authority to determine international environmental and labor policies remains to be seen—a proposal that is quite distinct from having the WTO recognize the existing standards of the ILO and the UN's environmental treaties on climate change, hazardous waste, the protection of biodiversity, ozone depletion, and so on. Some activists think the WTO's legislative and enforcement powers would strengthen environmental protections and trade union organizing. Others think the WTO would instead set limits on environmental regulations and labor rights, categorically defining them as "trade barriers" interfering with the so-called rights of corporations to pollute and exploit low-wage workers. Many Third World countries think WTO enforcement of rules governing labor and the environment would cripple their own economic development, to the advantage of the transnationals that can more readily invest in complying with such standards.

In fact, the Office of the High Commissioner for Human Rights at the UN has called the WTO "a nightmare for the poor, especially in the South" and found "apparent conflicts" between certain trade policies and the human rights to food, health, and self-determination. All in all, the legal relationship between the WTO and the UN system is one of the hottest topics on the international political horizon.

THE UN

Of all the international institutions, the UN is certainly the most democratic to date. One-country, one-vote is the fundamental decision-making principle, and diplomatic practice grants every country a virtual veto.

From April 25 to June 26, 1945, the drafters of the UN Charter met in San Francisco to assemble a document that had been already several years in the making with substantial public consultation, especially in the United States. At that time, there were just fifty nations; the architects of the UN building in New York City were told to plan for expansion to include perhaps seventy member states. As decades of decolonization allowed many more nations their independence—a process that continues to this day—the total UN membership has risen to more than 180 nations. While not a parliamentary system with direct proportionate representation, the one-country, one-vote principle has resulted in an institution in which the majority of the world's people have the majority of its voting rights. Some 140 "developing countries," where most of the world's poor reside, often work together as an effective voting bloc called the Group of 77, or G-77, harkening back to when there were seventy-seven of them.

Civil society groups, called nongovernmental organizations, or NGOs in UN-speak, have access to most UN deliberations, including the right to speak and submit papers. There is a formal process required to gain full "Consultative Status," but in response to the public's phenomenal interest in participating in the Earth Summit of 1992, as well as the other popular summits of the 1990s on human rights, women, population, habitat, and social development, the UN has made a great effort to include all interested NGOs in most of its meetings. In tricky negotiations, the decision whether or not to allow civil society representatives to be present has usually been left to the official chairperson of each particular session. While the chairs have varied in their receptivity, they often defer to the other governments present.

In contrast, the Security Council of the UN is very exclusive. It includes only fifteen members, of which just five enjoy permanent status—the others rotate. The five also possess exclusive veto power, referred to as "great power unanimity" within UN circles. The rationale at the time of its founding, with World War II a very recent memory, was that the great powers—the United States, United Kingdom, Soviet Union, China, and France— would not cooperate without reserving their right of military action. This legacy, however practical at the time, has prevented the Security Council from living up to its official charge: the maintenance of peace and the regulation of armaments.

Unfortunately, several of the permanent members have actively built up their military capacity throughout the decades. The United States has spent billions for preparations to wage war in several "theaters" at the same time, and by attacking Iraq in 2003, it demonstrated its willingness to unilaterally invade other countries under the guise of a "preventive" or "preemptive" attack.

Overall, the UN consists of six distinct "principal organs": the General Assembly, the Security Council, the Economic and Social Council (ECOSOC), the Trusteeship Council, the International Court of Justice, and the Secretariat. In addition, there are an array of other agencies, programs, and departments that report back to one or another of these organs.

For example, five regional commissions report to the ECOSOC, as do a variety of thematic commissions (for human rights, social development, the rights of women, and other high-profile issues) and a number of specialized agencies. The latter include the better known ILO, World Health Organization, and Food and Agriculture Organization as well as some less familiar bodies such as the International Telecommunications Union and the International Maritime Organization.

Some specialized agencies report to both ECOSOC and the General Assembly. These include the United Nations Environment Program, the UN Development Program, the UN Conference on Trade and Development, and the UN Children's Fund—perhaps better known by their initials: UNEP, UNDP, UNCTAD, and UNICEF respectively. A few less familiar specialized agencies reporting to both organs include the UN Center for Human Settlements and the UN University. Two specialized agencies reporting only to the General Assembly are the International Atomic Energy Agency and the UN Relief and Works Agency for Palestine Refugees in the Near East.

The specialized agencies have their own constitutions, memberships, and governing bodies, and they raise and allocate their own budgets, separate from the UN itself. The WTO, World Bank, and IMF are considered fully independent and connected by a dotted line with the rest of the UN in its published organizational chart, under the heading "related organizations." (See map below.)

Treaty bodies, which govern each of the many hundreds of international treaties developed under UN auspices, are also fully independent. Each new treaty must be ratified by willing nations, which then become responsible for all further treaty-related responsibilities—not only decision making and fund-raising, but the elaboration of legal protocols and other mechanisms to implement the agreements.

The organizational chart of the UN appears daunting, but in fact the bureaucracy is no greater than that of many states, cities, or universities. Slightly more than fifty thousand staff run the whole thing—about as many as are employed by the City of Stockholm or the State of Wyoming. The basic budget runs around $1.25 billion, similar to that of the University of Minnesota—although peacekeeping and humanitarian emergencies are accounted for separately, totaling up to as much as $10.5 billion in recent years. But even this amounts to less than 0.03 percent of the U.S. military budget. The UN has fewer committees and subcommittees than the U.S. Congress and, despite publishing most documents in six languages, consumes less paper in a year than the *New York Times* does on a single Sunday.

The UN's accomplishments are so extensive, it can be difficult to see the whole picture. In addition to peacekeeping, with more than 170 resolutions of regional conflicts to its credit, the UN has supervised elections in more than forty-five troubled countries. (Of course, no one thought to ask the world's ostensible beacon of democracy—or dared to ask them—to monitor the recent U.S. presidential election in which many improprieties

UNITED NATIONS

The UNITE

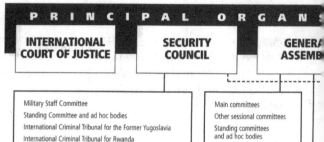

P R I N C I P A L   O R G A N S

INTERNATIONAL COURT OF JUSTICE

SECURITY COUNCIL

GENERA ASSEMB

Military Staff Committee

Standing Committee and ad hoc bodies

International Criminal Tribunal for the Former Yugoslavia

International Criminal Tribunal for Rwanda

UN Monitoring, Verification and Inspection Commission (Iraq)

United Nations Compensation Commission

Peacekeeping Operations and Missions

Main committees

Other sessional committees

Standing committees and ad hoc bodies

Other subsidiary organs

PROGRAMMES AND FUNDS

UNCTAD
United Nations Conference on Trade and Development

ITC
International Trade Centre (UNCTAD/WTO)

UNDCP
United Nations Drug Control Programme

UNEP
United Nations Environment Programme

UNHSP
United Nations Human Settlements Programme (UN-Habitat)

UNDP
United Nations Development Programme

UNIFEM
United Nations Development Fund for Women

UNV
United Nations Volunteers

UNFPA
United Nations Population Fund

UNHCR
Office of the United Nations High Commissioner for Refugees

UNICEF
United Nations Children's Fund

WFP
World Food Programme

UNRWA**
United Nations Relief and Works Agency for Palestine Refugees in the Near East

OTHER UN ENTITIES

OHCHR
Office of the United Nations High Commissioner for Human Rights

UNOPS
United Nations Office for Project Services

UNU
United Nations University

UNSSC
United Nations System Staff College

UNAIDS
Joint United Nations Programme on HIV/AIDS

RESEARCH AND TRAINING INSTITUTES

INSTRAW
International Research and Training Institute for the Advancement of Women

UNICRI
United Nations Interregional Crime and Justice Research Institute

UNITAR
United Nations Institute for Training and Research

UNRISD
United Nations Research Institute for Social Development

UNIDIR**
United Nations Institute for Disarmament Research

*Autonomous organizations working with the United Nations and each other through the coordinat

ATIONS system

ECONOMIC AND SOCIAL COUNCIL

TRUSTEESHIP COUNCIL

SECRETARIAT

IONAL COMMISSIONS

- on for Social Development
- on on Human Rights
- on on Narcotic Drugs
- on on Crime Prevention
  nal Justice
- on on Science and Technology
  pment
- on on Sustainable Development
- on on the Status of Women
- on on Population and
  ent
  Commission

NAL COMMISSIONS

- Commission for Africa (ECA)
- Commission for Europe (ECE)
- Commission for Latin America
  aribbean (ECLAC)
- and Social Commission for Asia
  acific (ESCAP)
- and Social Commission
  n Asia (ESCWA)

- ations Forum on Forests

- and Standing Committees
- l hoc and related bodies

ED ORGANIZATIONS

- nal Atomic Energy Agency

- ade)
  de Organization

- urism)
  rism Organization

- rep.com
  for the Nuclear-Test-Ban-Treaty
  on

- on for the Prohibition of
  Weapons

SPECIALIZED AGENCIES*

ILO
International Labour Organization

FAO
Food and Agriculture Organization
of the United Nations

UNESCO
United Nations Educational, Scientific
and Cultural Organization

WHO
World Health Organization

WORLD BANK GROUP

IBRD	International Bank for Reconstruction and Development
IDA	International Development Association
IFC	International Finance Corporation
MIGA	Multilateral Investment Guarantee Agency
ICSID	International Centre for Settlement of Investment Disputes

IMF
International Monetary Fund

ICAO
International Civil Aviation Organization

IMO
International Maritime Organization

ITU
International Telecommunication Union

UPU
Universal Postal Union

WMO
World Meteorological Organization

WIPO
World Intellectual Property Organization

IFAD
International Fund for Agricultural Development

UNIDO
United Nations Industrial Development
Organization

OSG
Office of the Secretary-General

OIOS
Office of Internal Oversight Services

OLA
Office of Legal Affairs

DPA
Department of Political Affairs

DDA
Department for Disarmament Affairs

DPKO
Department of Peacekeeping Operations

OCHA
Office for the Coordination
of Humanitarian Affairs

DESA
Department of Economic
and Social Affairs

DGACM
Department of General Assembly
and Conference Management

DPI
Department of Public Information

DM
Department of Management

OIP
Office of the Iraq Programme

UNSECOORD
Office of the United Nations
Security Coordinator

OHRLLS
Office of the High Representative
for the Least Developed Countries,
Landlocked Developing Countries
and Small Island Developing States

ODC
Office on Drugs and Crime

UNOG
UN Office at Geneva

UNOV
UN Office at Vienna

UNON
UN Office at Nairobi

Published by the United Nations

have been documented, especially in the state of Florida, governed by the victorious Bush's brother.)

The UN Development Program, with a budget of $1.3 billion, is the world's largest multilateral source of grants for development assistance, supporting some five thousand projects around the world. UNICEF spends $800 million a year on immunizations and other health care, nutrition, and basic education in 138 countries. The World Health Organization eradicated polio and small-pox from most of the world, and is working on malaria and other tropical diseases few drug companies bother to research. The ILO has achieved more than 183 separate conventions governing every conceivable aspect of labor standards. There are more than seventy human rights treaties, as well as innumerable investigations of torture and other cases of human rights abuse. Famine, natural disasters, nuclear proliferation, poverty, pollution, land mines, racism, and all the other scourges of humanity are doggedly attended to by the UN, with its modest staff and modest budget.

Civil society activists tend to be supportive of the UN and its overall agenda, although recent trends toward corporatization in the organization have been severely criticized. These include Secretary-General Kofi Annan's "Global Compact" with the business community, which appeals to, rather than requires, them to put into practice the principles of human, social, and environmental rights; the Johannesburg World Summit on Sustainable Development's promotion of "partnerships" with the private sector to supply what were previously public services, including the delivery of water and electricity; and the acceptance of funds for advertising—evidenced in their hanging a Coca-Cola banner over the entryway to a major UN conference. But the biggest failure most activists point to is the UN's inability to keep up: poverty, misery, and conflict continue to worsen worldwide.

Alas, the biggest reason is fairly simple: the United States has bucked the system. The United States has not participated in dozens of human rights and social development treaties, nor kept up with agreed targets for disarmament. Our government refuses to deal with global warming or bioweapons talks. It has not endorsed the International Criminal Court nor earlier treaties to handle terrorism. And it has never lived up to the goal of spending 0.7 percent of gross domestic product on foreign aid. Instead of sharing its wealth with the needy, the United States has periodically obtained reductions in its UN dues, required by international law and based on each country's gross domestic product (with downward adjustments for low per capita income or high foreign debt). By 1993, the United States owed more than $830 million in delinquent dues payments and refused to pay up for years, despite the fact that New York City alone benefits from some $800 million of yearly economic spending from hosting its headquarters.

In short, the UN system is fairly comprehensive and dedicated to equitable development, but it lacks support, especially from the world's richest and most powerful nation. It also lacks an effective enforcement mechanism with which to manage rogue nations (including the

United States), especially in comparison to the extremely powerful trade sanctions of the WTO and the conditionalities of the World Bank and IMF.

Part II

THE GLOBAL ECONOMY

For as long as humans have traveled, visitors have been received by locals with both gracious hospitality and suspicious hostility—depending upon the historical experience and the mission at hand. In recent decades, promises of expanded prosperity have proven false, although the rich are getting richer. Magnified by globalization, economic hardship and related social problems for the vast majority of people on this planet are not only contagious but spreading as fast as computerized money exchanges allow.

GLOBALIZATION

Back in the 1950s, U.S. Secretary of Defense Charlie Wilson remarked, "What's good for General Motors is good for the country," implying that government support for General Motors would trickle down into jobs and economic activity for U.S. citizens. Indeed, back in the 1930s, it was General Motors' president who coordinated the campaign to reallocate state and local highway tax revenues toward constructing the interstate highway system. Along with Standard Oil, the Greyhound Corporation, Firestone Tire, and Mack Truck, they eliminated six major railroads and the streetcar systems of forty-five cities. Convicted of antitrust violations in 1947, General Motors was fined just five thousand dollars.

Sure enough, during that postwar era, millions of families bought their first family car, the suburbs began to sprawl, and General Motors grew fat. Then, to make a long story very short, the oil companies and their host countries realized they had Americans "over a barrel," so to speak. In the 1970s, OPEC decided to quadruple the price of oil. Gasoline prices rose, and with the federal government devoting the nation's wealth to another war, this time in Vietnam, "stagflation"—a time of both economic stagnation and inflation—defined the era. The brief period of American optimism was over.

Worldwide, inflation also skyrocketed. Prices for everything, from gasoline and food to industrial equipment and wages, soared. Developing countries needed funds, and the banks were eager to lend "petro-dollars" from their bloated OPEC accounts. The World Bank, too, was rolling in petro-dollars, and issued a policy rewarding staff with promotions for pushing increased sums of money out the door. With little attention to a project's merit as an economic development strategy or to the credit-worthiness of its sponsors, the lenders scattered money around the world, almost indiscriminately. Even dictators were welcome to scoop up funds to pay off political friends and boost their illegal offshore accounts.

And the IMF provided still more loans, to keep debt payments flowing.

As loan portfolios ballooned everywhere, the IMF began to oblige indebted governments to raise taxes on food, gasoline, and other basic commodities, and to cut back on health and education, all in order to funnel cash back to the creditors. It also began to require a devaluing of the national currency. So if, for example, a peso once was enough to buy a bushel of corn, it would now buy only part of a bushel. This is tough on local people; their paychecks and savings are suddenly worth less. But it's great for exporters, whose corn or oil or diamonds are suddenly cheaper compared to their overseas competitors; they can sell a lot more, making up in volume what they lost in value.

While all this exporting brings in a certain amount of foreign exchange to pay off debts, there's nothing in this scheme to guarantee that increased economic activity trickles down to local people. In fact, it doesn't. Rioting occurred in Argentina, Jamaica, Venezuela, Ghana, the Philippines, Indonesia, and numerous other countries that bore witness to the hardship and popular revolt caused by IMF-imposed structural adjustment policies.

The so-called development projects financed by the World Bank tend to be environmentally destructive, too, while profiting corporate developers. The great dams, for example, destroy massive ecosystems and disrupt hydrological cycles with severe and long-term impacts—not to mention the displacement of millions of people. Some 20 percent of all the World Bank's lending goes to the energy sector, but for each dollar spent on renewable sources, twenty-five dollars are spent on fossil fuels. It's as if they've never heard of climate change!

And then there is all the waste, much of it toxic, accumulating as a result of Western consumer lifestyles. All the polluting by-products on the production side and the disposable trash on the consumer side add up to gargantuan environmental problems. And alas, it is the poor who suffer most immediately from environmental contamination: they live right where the poisons accumulate, as corporations emit wastes and otherwise dump in poor neighborhoods, while the rich are quick to move away.

Numerous treaties—known collectively as Multilateral Environmental Agreements, or MEAs—have been negotiated under UN auspices over the decades, to grapple with the fearful consequences of the modern industrial model of development. The UN's first summit on the environment took place in Stockholm in 1972. Over the next twenty years, dozens of treaties were born covering pollution at sea, tropical forests, the ozone layer, hazardous waste, endangered species and other wildlife, specific vulnerable regions including the Amazon and Antarctica, and so on. In 1992, the Earth Summit in Rio de Janeiro generated two new MEAs: the Framework Convention on Climate Change and the Convention on Biological Diversity. Since then, a number of additional treaties have been achieved. And in some cases, detailed implementation treaties, known as protocols, have been penned to help reach the goals expressed more generally in the original convention. But the ten-year review conference of the

Rio Earth Summit, held in Johannesburg, South Africa, was perceived by many civil society groups as a failure—a barren attempt on the part of our governments to pretend that all this treaty making had accomplished something, while pollution and biological destruction continue virtually unchecked.

In the cities, epidemiologists have identified the industrial causes of conditions such as cancer, heart disease, diabetes, infertility, and birth defects. Corporate scientists often claim that a person's genetic heritage is to blame, but our genes only bear the brunt of the poisons. Each of us may have inherited greater resistance to certain environmental toxins or greater vulnerability to others, but, in either case, our bodies—our genes—are responding to external factors. And in rural areas, food security often depends upon the local productive capacity: the next harvest is hurt by soil erosion and degradation, deforestation and desertification, the rechanneling of rivers, declining biological diversity, and drought. Toxic pesticides and fertilizers, too, have poisoned millions of rural people; and, sadly, these chemicals are used all too often in desperate acts of suicide by those who give up struggling for a better life.

Many countries that once produced their own basic foods are now dependent on expensive imports, having switched to export production under IMF conditions of structural adjustment and in accord with "free trade" policies. Kenya, for example, became a net importer of corn, their major staple food crop, after the structural adjustment and trade liberalization of the 1990s. Corn farmers lost about half the value of their production while their costs, mostly for imported fertilizers, rose. With the privatization of Kenya's National Cereals and Produce Board, the government's ability to manage the supply of corn and keep prices stable was greatly reduced, leaving Kenya's food security dependent upon imports and transnational commercial interests.

In Mexico, NAFTA cut the value of Mexican corn farmers' crops in half, while doubling the cost of agricultural inputs. In the Mexican countryside, the highly touted transition from basic grains to horticulture failed: vegetables intended for export never became competitive in the world market, while corn imports from the United States increased by a factor of eighteen. Flooded with corn, prices for producers fell drastically, and yet, with corporate production overwhelming the smaller, family-owned tortilla businesses in urban areas, the price of tortillas actually went up! As a whole, the economy of the rural sector shrank by 6 percent in 1997, despite Mexico's gross domestic product growing by 7 percent.

The Philippines, formerly food self-sufficient, now depends upon imported rice to feed its population, after being made to shift from family subsistence and market plots to plantation sugar, oil palm, and (ironically) rice production for the export market, all thanks to structural adjustment and the GATT/WTO. Similar stories can be told of nation upon nation.

The WTO Agreement on Agriculture obliges countries to import certain percentages of foods, whether or not they need them. Yet a parallel WTO agreement (the

Marrakesh Decision] that promised to provide instant aid for those least-developed and net food-importing countries negatively affected by the agriculture agreement has never been implemented: that is because the IMF argued these poor countries couldn't *prove* their food security problems were a direct result of the WTO.

But globalization, trade rules, international loans, structural adjustment, and environmental exploitation work well for the corporate sector. Under trade rules, countries have to treat the exporting companies of all other nations just as they treat their own companies. Great! The big transnationals have access to every country that joins the WTO! The World Bank finances harbors and roads and dams. Great! This is just the infrastructure transnational companies need to exploit a country's natural resources and bring them to export markets. And the IMF keeps priming the pump. Great! Squeeze those economies so the big money can trickle back to the headquarters of Citigroup, Goldman-Sachs, and the other financial giants in New York City, London, and Zurich.

Today, General Motors is the third-ranked company on the Global 500 list, with $184.6 billion in revenues. Its president makes $4.8 million a year, while an average autoworker makes $23 an hour. In the average Fortune 200 company, top executives make about $10 million, while roughly half of the entire U.S. workforce earns less than $60,000. Globally, the average income of hardworking people is rapidly eroding further.

CONTAGION

In Asia during the 1960s, 1970s, and 1980s, the more economically successful governments actively managed their own affairs. They invested in job creation, regulated capital flows and financial markets, and supported national enterprises and exporting into the global market. Overall, the region thrived with better growth rates than even the United States. The trouble came, says Nobel Prize winner Joseph Stiglitz, when the Thai government succumbed to IMF and U.S. Treasury pressure and agreed to deregulate its financial and capital markets.

Until then, Thailand had restricted bank lending for speculative real estate, preferring that available capital be invested in job creation. With restrictions lifted, new money poured into the country, spurring a speculative real estate boom; but it all collapsed when investors realized the debt load was unsustainable and more attractive interest rates could be found elsewhere in the world. By the late 1990s, this "hot money," as short-term investments are called, fled not only Thailand but also other East Asian countries, and the economic crisis spread in what became known as "Asian contagion." Eventually, the panic spread all the way to Russia and Brazil as global investors chose to avoid risky economies altogether.

In any recession, it is the poor who suffer most. Thailand's rural poor, who had flocked into the cities during the boom years, were left without a safety net; the lucky ones returned home to their villages, where at least food and shelter could be found. But the global institutions' response, funded by U.S. taxpayers, was directed toward making the banking system whole again—lending money at very favorable rates to the IMF to lend in turn to the central banks in Asia, which then lent to insolvent companies to pay off their creditors, which tended to be the major international banks. The U.S.-orchestrated bailout did nothing for the poor.

Since 1995, the IMF, World Bank, and U.S. Treasury have put together at least eight other bailouts (in Asia as well as in Russia, Mexico, and Brazil), transferring $250 billion worth of risk from the balance sheets of banks and other companies to the public sector and the multilateral system. All in all, this process generates a tidy shift of resources from the public to private interests, and from poor to rich.

Argentina's crisis at the turn of the century was provoked by the global downturn following the Asian crisis, but it had been building for decades. Since joining the IMF in 1956, Argentina had borrowed funds in thirty-four out of forty-five years and cooperated with all of the structural adjustments required—including nationalizing private debt incurred during the dictatorship and encouraging foreign ownership of the banking system. By 2001, the government owed more than $200 billion in debt—more than $160 billion to private foreign banks including Chase Manhattan, J.P. Morgan, and Citigroup, and about $25 billion to the IMF, World Bank, and other public lenders.

In 2000, a judge in the federal criminal court found a history of unscrupulous mismanagement of the country's finances and declared that since 1976, Argentina had been "placed at the mercy of external creditors, and in those negotiations IMF officials participated actively." Judge Jorge Ballestero emphasized that the effect was "to benefit private companies and businesses—both national and foreign—to the prejudice of state companies that suffered policies impoverishing them further every day." He specified, among other things, that the governor of Argentina's central bank, Domingo Cavallo, in 1982 near the end of the military dictatorship, created public guarantees insuring $17 billion of private debt and a number of foreign loans to private domestic companies—effectively nationalizing this debt. By 2001, the part of the nationalized debt incurred by the dictatorship had grown to some $43 billion, more than one-fifth of the country's total debt.

Domingo Cavallo has a long résumé. In 1991, serving his country as Argentina's finance minister, he pegged the Argentine peso to the U.S. dollar—meaning that Argentina's central bank could no longer manage its value according to Argentine economic and political factors; instead, their currency's value would automatically rise and fall with the value of the dollar. The theory was that foreign investors would appreciate the security of the dollar and bring funds into the country. Also during that period, Argentina joined Brazil, Uruguay, and Paraguay in a regional economic development plan called Mercosur, or "Market of the South," designed to boost cooperation in the region and increase its capacity relative to the rest of the world.

At first, money did pour in as investors scrambled to buy up Argentine dollar bonds and pieces of the country's privatized power and communications sectors. But Brazil's currency was not pegged to the dollar, and instead of buying wheat in overvalued Argentinean money from its Mercosur partner Argentina, Brazil bought it from the United States. Within one year, Argentina's trade deficit exceeded $1.2 billion. In desperation, the Carlos Menem administration announced it would give tax refunds for exporters, eliminate domestic duties on farm exports, fuel oil and diesel oil, and set higher import tariffs. In a speech one month later, Domingo Cavallo hinted that he thought regional integration was impossible and that joining NAFTA might be preferable to instability within Mercosur.

But stability in Mexico was not to be had, either. Even before IMF intervention, the Mexican economy had already suffered decades of manipulation by the dominant political party, the Partido Revolucionario Institutional (PRI). For many decades, the PRI controlled the presidency, and their six-year terms were usually marked by early austerity. While this improved the country's financial balances, pleasing the international community, the subsequent steep drop in real wages, onset of recession, and increased income inequality displeased voters. So midterm, presidents would start redistributing income through subsidies and other public investments, gaining popular support in time for the next election but displeasing the banks.

Then in 1984, the IMF bailed out the Mexican economy with a deal persuading the commercial banks to leave their money in the country in exchange for an IMF-designed structural adjustment program. Simultaneously, the World Bank for the first time went beyond its mandate to finance development projects and joined in debt-related lending. A few years later, the banks invented the Baker Plan—named after U.S. Treasury Secretary James Baker, who served under the Reagan administration—and convinced both private and public sector banks to increase their loans in Mexico (and a dozen other countries) in exchange for structural adjustment, tax reform, intervention in labor markets, and further trade and investment liberalization. Baker's successor at Treasury, Nicholas Brady, then sweetened the deal for the banks. The Brady Plan offered stronger international guarantees to cover the risks of all those new loans, in exchange for which the banks would forgive part of the principal and accept lower interest rates on the balances. Debt instruments began to trade in secondary and tertiary markets, as the banks holding potentially bad loans sold them at discounted rates to others who were either more optimistic or figured they could make money off the public guarantees.

Meanwhile, a remarkable coalition of creditors invented an array of legal and accounting devices to maintain as much of the full value of the debt as possible. Canada, France, Germany, and the United Kingdom recategorized funds kept in reserve for potential loan losses as tax deductible. Japan created tax deductions for one percent of all capital tied up in risk reserves. The head of the U.S. Federal Reserve Bank at the time, Paul Volcker, informed U.S. banks that if they complied with the Brady Plan they would "not be subject to supervisory criticism." The UN Center on Transnational Corporations documented twenty-three tax and accounting incentives developed by governments to support the private banks during that period.

For a while, Mexico was a star performer in the Baker-Brady scheme for debt restructuring, and according to the established routine, the PRI again won the presidency, putting Carlos Salinas in office in 1988. Under Salinas, Mexico's total debt climbed from $70 billion in 1989 to $100 billion by 1992. Foreign investments, too, had climbed, encouraged by Salinas's active pursuit of the NAFTA agreement, but most of this wealth was invested in services, tourism, and foreign ownership of Mexican assets.

As the vote on NAFTA approached in the U.S. Congress, the peso-to-dollar exchange rate began to fluctuate wildly. Salinas used the government's stock of foreign currency to buy pesos, tightening the money supply in hopes of sustaining the peso's value until the next presidential election. In the last week before the November 17, 1993 NAFTA vote, as Bill Clinton brokered billions of dollars' worth of political deals with congressional representatives to ensure a "yes" vote, investors pulled $5 billion out of Mexico fearing a "no." Salinas allowed the exchange rate to rise, so investors would have to exchange more pesos to get their dollars out, and currency exchange shops on the border stopped accepting pesos altogether.

The Salinas administration increased interest rates, hoping to lure investors back, and when the U.S. Congress approved NAFTA, the peso did not crash. In August 1994, the PRI Party once again won the Mexican presidency, putting Ernesto Zedillo in office.

But four months later, the peso crashed. The Mexican treasury had run out of dollar reserves with which to buy up pesos to keep them out of the money supply, thus they could no longer prop up their scarcity value. Bill Clinton agreed to a bailout by U.S. taxpayers, supplying a $40 billion line of credit, and the IMF added $18 billion, but the peso continued to fall—from a ratio of three to the dollar before the NAFTA vote to seven to the dollar. This meant that paychecks and savings in Mexico were worth less than half their value compared to the glory days when NAFTA was signed, while the real cost of food and other necessities doubled. The crumbling peso caused panic to spread throughout Latin America.

What resulted has been called the "tequila effect," as investors scrambled to withdraw their funds from what they feared were low-end financial markets. And the tequila effect had particularly harsh effects in Argentina, which lost $8 billion in capital flight and spent $7 billion in reserves to balance the exchange value of its currency. By midyear, Brazil devalued its currency twice, threatened to limit its imports of Argentine automobiles, and entertained proposals from Brazilian wheat millers to drop the Mercosur tariff on wheat imposed from outside the region. Argentina found itself unable to compete.

Then in 1995, the United States raised interest rates, forcing the value of the Argentine currency to rise as well. This meant Argentina's exports became even more expensive, relative to its trading partners in Europe and Brazil, and imports cheaper. So export revenues fell while cheaper imports flooded the domestic market, driving out domestic production. People lost jobs. When Brazil devalued its currency in 1998, the problem grew worse. The loss of foreign exchange—through diminishing export revenues and payments for growing imports—reached critical proportions while unemployment rose to double digits. And then the Asian crisis raised interest rates globally, augmenting the cost of servicing Argentina's debt while investors both foreign and domestic sent their money to safer economies.

In 1999, Carlos Menem left the presidency, discredited for overissuing dollar bonds to finance budgetary deficits and accused of corruption. Since then, a series of Argentine presidents have tried to rebuild the economy through desperate tactics—suspending payments on the debt, decoupling the currency from the dollar, and prohibiting bank withdrawals to prevent any further capital flight. Without cash and without jobs, millions of middle-class Argentines are suffering a frightening slide into poverty.

With links to the Asian contagion (not to mention decades of dictators and engagement with the IMF and World Bank), Argentina's economic crisis spread to Uruguay, Brazil, and throughout Latin America. It is increasingly apparent: the more globalized the economy, the more contagious our economic problems—and the social problems thereof.

Even in the United States, the middle class is shrinking and economic issues rank very high on the political agenda. So far, our government has managed to insulate most of us from the terrors of extreme poverty—although declining tax revenues and skyrocketing military budgets threaten those minimal protections that our government provides the poor. Since the Welfare Reform Act of 1996, nearly half of all food stamp recipients have been eliminated from the program due to its more rigorous eligibility standards, and some 23 million people had to go to Second Harvest and other private sources for food aid in 2001. Some 40 million people, more than 14 percent of the U.S. population, lacked health insurance during the past few years.

Is our social order really "sound as a dollar"? How sound is the U.S. dollar, anyway? How do all these economic factors—currency exchange rates, interest rates, the money supply, trade balances, and foreign investment—affect us in the wealthiest nation on Earth? In fact, how did we get to be the wealthiest nation in the first place?

MONEY

Five hundred years ago, explorers paid no more than shipping costs to extract slaves, gold, silver, and other precious raw materials to their home country to be sold at fabulous prices. Since the prohibition of slavery, low-wage labor to manufacture goods made out of imported raw materials has enriched the industrialized world while the providers of this expropriated wealth have suffered in poverty. In short, labor and natural resources— the resources of the Third World (often referred to as "the South") have always been abundant, undervalued, and exploited.

Of course, labor and natural resources in the industrialized world (also called "the North") have also been exploited and undervalued. But there have always been more wealthy entrepreneurs in the North ready to invest in extracting value from the South than vice versa— resulting in a historical problem that has affected geopolitics ever since.

Over the centuries, industrialization and capital accumulation in the North have created a pattern of trade where developing countries sell natural resources to traders from the industrialized world, and then import those same materials in the form of processed goods. Despite modernization, this fundamental disequilibrium in the exchange rate of the respective resources between the South and the North is actually worsening. The technical term for this relationship is the "terms of trade," and analysts have declared them to be "deteriorating" for decades—despite the stated intentions of the World Bank, IMF, and GATT/WTO. Countries exporting coffee and cocoa, jute and pineapple, timber, copper, and bauxite have watched their value on the commodity exchanges plummet year after year, while the prices of the pesticides and tractors, factories, refrigeration, and modern mining equipment they import rise. The more technology adds costs and presumed efficiencies to the up-front costs of their imports, the more developing countries' terms of trade deteriorate.

When Argentina exports beef to the United States, it brings in dollars; when it exports to Japan, it brings in yen. Theoretically, the dollars go back to the United States when Argentines import Fords and the yen go back to Japan when they import Toyotas. Of course, trade balances are never perfect, so surpluses of one currency and deficits of another can accumulate.

Over time, each government's economic planners are supposed to strive toward a "balance of trade" with other countries while the central bankers are supposed to try to maintain a "balance of payments" in all currencies. This can be done, in part, by keeping currency reserves in stock—to buy back the national currency from other countries' central banks when a domestic shortage is on the horizon, and to release funds into the domestic economy when necessary to stabilize the money supply relative to demand. All of this, in theory, keeps the value of money steady, preventing inflation and maintaining sound economies.

However, a variety of factors interfere with the smooth functioning of supply and demand in the international economy. For one thing, central banks in each country adjust their "money supply" and thus the value of their money every day. These adjustments at many national levels may contradict each other and exacerbate the conditions they were intended to correct. They also stimulate human behaviors that can be difficult to accurately calibrate in advance, with economic responses that take months to filter through the system.

When the chair of the Federal Reserve Bank lowers interest rates by 0.25 percent, it makes money cheaper to access, so it encourages people to borrow more. In the United States, consumer credit is so incredibly extensive that many of us often receive loan offers in the mail. Greenspan and the other economic planners want us to spend our borrowed money—on cars, furniture, new homes, jeans, and CDs—and thus keep the economy going. When we're all out there buying stuff, the economy thrives: manufacturers produce more, retailers build up their inventory, and the furniture and car dealers and realtors raise their prices. If this goes on too long, people start worrying about inflation (prices rising faster than wages and other values in the economy) and then decide they can no longer afford all these goods. Then the banks tighten the money supply, raising interest rates so that people will put their money in the bank instead of buying so much stuff, and the economy shrinks. When people are pinching pennies and retailers are overstocked, prices go down and inflation falls. Every country's money supply constantly fluctuates, so as goods are traded and currencies exchanged internationally, surprises and volatility are the norm in the global economy.

Another glitch in the balancing of trade and payments internationally is the fact that at least one third of all world trade is conducted by transnational corporations buying and selling goods between their own affiliates in different countries. As you might expect, corporations charge prices designed to benefit the bottom line. In particular, taxes can be avoided by overpricing goods sold to U.S.-based affiliates from operations based overseas and underpricing goods sold to overseas affiliates from operations based in the United States. For example, in 2000, a study by finance professors at the University of Florida found a $2,306 hypodermic syringe and a $1.58 ton of soybeans. How about a $528 bulldozer and a $5,655 toothbrush? While each firm can balance its discounts and premiums to ensure internal accuracy, the practice—known as "transfer pricing"—keeps the income out of its reports to the Internal Revenue Service. Transfer pricing is entirely legal; international accounting firms even advertise their expertise with transfer pricing to attract clients. But it can certainly screw up national accounts!

A third destabilizing factor in the global economy is the relatively recent decoupling of money from anything of real worth. The U.S. dollar may be considered the most stable currency in the world, but (hard to believe) it is not worth anything more today than the trust we give it. Until 1974, the U.S. dollar was formally based on the "gold standard"; anyone could trade in their paper money for gold from the vaults in Fort Knox. While no one can eat gold, it and other precious metals have had a relatively stable value in world markets over the centuries. Under the gold standard, the currencies of other countries were fixed at agreed ratios to the dollar and also redeemable for gold at that rate. But the United States began to accumulate a dollar deficit in the 1960s, with heavy expenditures on the Vietnam War, and the flow of dollars to higher-interest investments overseas accelerated with President Nixon's effort to stimulate the economy through lower interest rates. By 1971, foreign claims on the gold stored in Fort Knox were double the value of the actual stock of gold. The Nixon administration unilaterally devalued the dollar and temporarily stopped payments in gold for dollars in foreign exchange. Then, with a stroke of the pen, Nixon permanently divorced the dollar from the gold standard, and currencies everywhere were decoupled from their foundation in real wealth.

Nowadays, the value of the dollar—as well as that of every other currency, gold and silver, and any other commodity traded in the formal commodities markets—flickers from microsecond to microsecond to the digitized pulse of computer software packages across the globe. These computer calculations tally their investors' returns down to a ten-thousandth of a dollar, based on minute advantages to be found in the vacillating interest rates and exchange rates from one country to another. Each incremental sliver of profit is then reinvested instantly, yielding exponentially expanding wealth based on nothing more than all the other investors' simultaneous behavior. Occasionally, the data on all these computers will prompt investment advisors to move their clients' funds out of a particular country's currency altogether, and the sudden rushing outflow of this hot money can leave that country devastated.

The investors then have to rush into another economy with their capital, although they have no intention of investing long-term; their computers are just looking for the next ten-thousandth of an incremental gain. Such short-term investments in currency exchange markets are not linked to real production of any kind: no factory is built, no streets or water treatment facilities are constructed, no value-added processing occurs, no technology or technological know-how is transferred—and so there is no real economic development. Or funds may be poured into speculative real estate development, but when the bubble bursts and investors decide to pull out, the gigantic cement forms for office towers are abandoned mid-construction, highway projects dead-end, and thousands of people lose their jobs.

As if international supply and demand, transfer pricing, hot money, and speculative real estate aren't unpredictable enough, investment advisors have invented an array of speculative financial instruments based on the future movement of exchange rates, interest rates, and mixed portfolios of stocks. From 1960 to 1990, trading in these high-risk "futures" and even more complex "derivatives" of these financial instruments increased some 700 percent, far outpacing the value of trade in actual goods and services. Essentially a gamble on future prices of all these dynamic interrelated instruments, speculation—performed by only a small number of trading companies—can make (or lose) money whether prices rise or fall; it merely depends on the accuracy of speculators' guesses. Volatility itself became remunerative for the gamblers, while the negative effects on consumers and small producers as well as whole economies are suffered worldwide.

Enron specialized in this global pyramid scheme, which is not illegal, trading in speculative derivatives financed by shareholders with layer over layer of paper deals, and anticipating future gains by betting electronically on the value held in its employees' retirement funds. The big banks, J.P. Morgan, Chase, and Citigroup, have been implicated in the deception. Insider trading, fraudulent accounting, and other illegal activities resulted in criminal charges and the incarceration of Enron executives. And Enron's auditor, the since discredited and now defunct Andersen company, let it all happen. Indeed, the global corruption watchdogs at Transparency International (http://www.transparency.org) cite Enron and the other corporate scandals of that period as garnering the United States its high corruption rating in their 2002 index; ranked sixteenth, the United States was deemed more corrupt than nine European countries, Iceland, Canada, New Zealand and Australia, Singapore, and Hong Kong.

Presumably, the Securities and Exchange Commission (SEC) of the United States and similar market oversight agencies of other countries have some responsibility for approving financial instruments and deals, and for supervising the accounting profession. Two years before Enron's collapse, the SEC tried to limit consulting between companies and their auditors, but the political heat from corporate lobbyists was intense and the stronger regulations failed. Under the Bush administration, SEC Commissioner Harvey Pitts (who used to represent the big accounting firms in his law practice) tried to privatize this responsibility and prompted the mass resignation of a five-member ethics board that oversees the accounting profession. After Enron's collapse, Pitts appointed William Webster, former director of both the FBI and the CIA, to take on this responsibility, adding to the public dissatisfaction with his leadership. Webster survived in this position just a few months, and by the end of 2002, Pitts himself resigned in disgrace.

In the wake of the scandals at Enron, Andersen, WorldCom, Adelphia, ImClone, and other major companies, it seemed that the demand for accountability from corporate executives and reforms of the accounting and auditing systems, derivatives markets, and the financing of political campaigns might lead to genuine reforms. But the Republicans' success in the 2002 midterm elections for Congress gave President Bush's corporate and militarist agenda a green light. Whether there is enough political will to alter our approach to terms of trade, international investments and financing in the near term is doubtful—especially in times of war, when citizens become reluctant to rock an already unsteady boat.

The juxtaposition of economic contraction and military expansion is a familiar scenario, however, and raises the question: Who benefits?

Part III

CORPORATE POLITICS

In today's world, most governments are led by an elite class with the resources to influence and dominate the political process. Historically, this is certainly true and nowhere more true than in the United States. For those with a global reach, trade policy has been seen as a particularly effective way to force other countries to open up their markets to major corporations—at least since the Truman administration blocked congressional ratification of the ITO's comprehensive approach that would have embraced the goals of full employment, respect for labor rights, and other elements of "fair trade." During the seventies, the GATT added "nontariff barriers" to its agenda, limiting the kinds of rules governments could make to control the quantity and quality of imports. But it was the Reagan administration that, hand in hand with corporate advisors, devised NAFTA and the WTO—nearly perfect instruments for the globalization of corporate power.

CORPORATE INFLUENCE

Corporate influence in the White House is rampant.

U.S. President George W. Bush and his Texan family are deeply invested in oil and other energy companies. Vice President Dick Cheney, who served as the first President Bush's secretary of defense, was the chief executive in another diversified energy corporation, the Halliburton Energy Company, which enjoyed $23.8 million in contracts to rebuild Iraq's oil fields after the Gulf War of 1991. Halliburton now has an exclusive contract to supply logistics for both the national army and navy. Donald Rumsfeld, now President Bush's defense secretary, was President Reagan's envoy to Iraq in 1983, charged with gaining Saddam Hussein's support against Iran, where the fundamentalists in power were perceived as a threat to U.S. oil interests in the region. The U.S. spent billions building up Hussein's military capability and supported his side (not to mention his opponents) in the Iran-Iraq war over five long years. Two decades later, the U.S. economy and our frontline soldiers are suffering the consequences of this buildup, as we switch our geopolitical perception of "the enemy" while Halliburton and the rest of the energy industry continue to profit.

Even so, corporate influence extends well beyond the energy sector. Donald Rumsfeld served as president of Searle Pharmaceuticals before it merged with chemical giant Monsanto; and our present secretary of agriculture, Anne Venemen, used to serve with Calgene, a biotech company subsequently bought up by Monsanto. Environmental Protection Agency Deputy Administrator Linda Fisher came to the Bush administration from

Monsanto, where she served as chief lobbyist in Washington.

During a period of rising militarism, does it surprise anyone that the U.S. government promotes Monsanto, other agribusiness and biotech companies, and the pharmaceutical and energy industries in both our domestic and foreign policies?

At least the Enron debacle has revealed to the world how deeply corporate interests have penetrated our government. Nearly everyone knows that Enron ranked as the biggest contributor to the campaign to elect President George W. Bush and that as many as thirty-five high-level Bush administration officials were former Enron officials or big-time investors. The company then enjoyed a $254 million tax rebate from the U.S. Treasury in 2001 before depriving its employees of their retirement benefits, investors of their savings, and going bankrupt.

Enron's influence not only corrupted our democracy at home, but also overseas. For example, Vice President Dick Cheney met with the president of India's Congress Party in 2001 to discuss the future of a $2.9 billion power plant owned primarily by Enron. The Maharashtra state utility company that bought about two thirds of the plant's production had stopped payments on grounds that Enron's prices were out of line. It's probably not a coincidence that, just around that time, the White House energy policy was amended to direct the State Department and the Department of Energy to "help India maximize its domestic oil and gas production." Similarly, when Mozambican officials rejected an Enron deal to develop a huge natural gas reservoir there, the U.S. Embassy applied pressure, threatening to withdraw U.S. aid from this poorest country in Africa if they didn't cooperate. Enron operated in many other countries as well, and was cited by Human Rights Watch for violations of international human rights as set out by the UN.

But don't think for a minute that the Bush family or the Republican Party is alone in wielding corporate power from the White House.

Tyson Foods, one of the world's largest poultry- and meat-processing companies, based in Arkansas, was a major supporter of Bill Clinton's presidential campaign as well as his earlier campaigns for the governorship of Arkansas. This is hardly surprising, as Tyson stands to gain mightily from the opening of trade with China and the lifting of tariffs on livestock and meat products under NAFTA in 2003—both deals negotiated by the Clinton administration. After Tyson's influence on White House policy was exposed, Clinton's Secretary of Agriculture Michael Espy resigned in disgrace.

Vice President Al Gore, serving with Bill Clinton, hired a former lobbyist for the Genentech biotech company to be his chief domestic policy advisor. Robert Rubin, secretary of the treasury during the Clinton administration, became chairman of the executive committee of the Citigroup bank that lent Enron hundreds of millions of dollars. Mickey Kantor, Clinton's secretary of commerce and U.S. trade representative, joined the Monsanto board of directors on his way out the "revolving door" of the White House.

In 1986, then-president Reagan appointed a lifetime executive of the Cargill Company, Daniel Amstutz, to represent our country in the agriculture talks in the GATT negotiations that created the WTO. Is anyone surprised that Cargill's empire and the reach of other transnational agribusiness companies have expanded dramatically since then? Also in the name of the U.S. citizenry, the Reagan administration embraced a self-appointed Intellectual Property Committee of pharmaceutical and agribusiness companies that drafted what was later codified as the WTO Agreement on Trade-Related Intellectual Property Rights (TRIPS). No surprise here, either, that the global drug and biotech-chemical corporations are now happily filing patents to monopolize these sectors in countries that formerly produced more affordable medicines and locally adapted seeds for themselves. Reagan's appointee to the Office of the U.S. Trade Representative, Clayton Yeutter, has since moved on to the board of directors of Mycogen Corporation, a part of the Dow Chemical Company.

For administration after administration, the White House and corporate lobbyists have used trade negotiations to pry open the global economy for the benefit of giant commercial interests. And administration after administration has tried to persuade Congress to give up its constitutional responsibility to oversee international trade relations. The infamous "fast-track" legislation, officially called Trade Promotion Authority, eliminates congressional oversight of WTO and other trade negotiations, substituting instead a simple "yes" or "no" vote over immensely complicated final packages made up of hundreds of deals, each affecting the environment, jobs, and our economy. Well-organized citizen campaigns in just about every state succeeded in defeating this legislation numerous times over the years, but in August 2002, by a narrow margin of 215–212 in the House and 66–34 in the Senate, the Congress finally gave up our tidbit of democratic access to these international economic decisions.

With this unchecked power in hand, the White House hastens to pursue the corporate agenda through numerous trade negotiations—at least until June 2005, when this "fast track" expires and the authority of our representatives in Congress is renewed.

INVESTORS' RIGHTS

The most insidious move yet empowering global corporations is enshrined in NAFTA's Chapter 11—and it is one that has been aggressively pushed by the U.S. trade representative in every other ongoing trade negotiation since its inception. This Chapter 11 (not to be confused with U.S. bankruptcy law) gives corporations the right to sue governments when their regulations interfere with the corporations' right to make money. Unnoticed by critics during the NAFTA negotiations, Chapter 11 has restructured democracy, sovereignty, and constitutional law, affecting the powers of the three countries' federal, state, and municipal governments.

Chapter 11 broadens the concept of protecting private

property from "takings," stating that no government may "directly or indirectly nationalize or expropriate an investment...or take a measure tantamount to nationalization or expropriation." In particular, the words "indirectly" and "tantamount to" are exceedingly vague. When the Mexican negotiator at the time complained that the scope was so broad it could lead to unintended effects, the United States offered its own frail reassurance that "the ebb and flow of arbitral wisdom would contribute to reasonably limit its scope."

Let's see how wisely and reasonably Chapter 11 has performed. When the Mexican state of San Luis Potosi denied a permit application for a hazardous waste facility on a stream, on grounds that public health and the environment would be harmed, the U.S. waste company Metalclad filed a Chapter 11 claim. Even though Metalclad hadn't bothered to file for the permit until the facility was nearly complete, the company argued that the town's response, declaring the area an ecological preserve, was tantamount to an expropriation. The NAFTA tribunal decided in favor of Metalclad, requiring Mexican taxpayers to pay the firm $16 million in compensation.

In 1998, Canadian taxpayers paid Ethyl, a company in California, $13 million to settle a Chapter 11 suit. Ethyl claimed Canada's ban on the import of its neurotoxic gasoline additive expropriated $250 million in future profits. The settlement also required lifting the ban and, to add insult to injury, a public statement to the effect that MMT, the manganese-based additive, was neither a health nor environmental risk.

The tables were turned when a Canadian company named Methanex sued the United States for $970 million, arguing that California's phaseout of its carcinogenic gasoline additive MTBE was an expropriation of that company's anticipated profits. Studies have identified ten thousand possible sites where MTBE is leaking into the groundwater, and cleanup costs could reach $1 million each. This case is pending. "We find it disconcerting," wrote fourteen members of the California legislature, "that our democratic decision making regarding this important public health issue is being second-guessed in a distant forum by unelected officials."

Here are a few other actual cases generated under these investors' rights provisions in NAFTA:

➤ S.D. Myers, a U.S. company, objected to a 1995Canadian law implementing an international treaty called the Basel Convention on Hazardous Wastes that banned exports of PCB waste. The ban was revoked in 1997, but the NAFTA tribunal awarded the company $8.2 million compensation for lost income.

➤ SunBelt Water is another U.S. company suing Canada, in this case for between $1 billion and $10.5 billion after losing its bid in a British Columbia court to export bulk freshwater.

➤ A Canadian company named Mondev is suing U.S. taxpayers for $16 million after the City of Boston denied its request for a permit to build a shopping mall back in the 1980s—this is despite a Massachusetts law protecting the city's Redevelopment Authority from liability.

➤ Tobacco giant Philip Morris is suing Canada for prohibiting the words "light and mild" on cigarette packages.

➤ Perhaps most outrageously, United Parcel Service is suing Canada on grounds its national postal service competes unfairly with the private sector!

Clearly, the investors' rights of Chapter 11 in NAFTA has gone far beyond the "reasonable" test and must be revoked.

Another approach to investors' rights can be found in "procurement" rules, established in both NAFTA and the WTO. These rules cover how governments buy materials such as pencils, paper, computers, and contracted services. Like Chapter 11, they extend the rights of investors while limiting the rights of national, regional, state, and local governments. Trade rules for procurement applying the National Treatment and Most Favored Nation concepts make it illegal for local authorities to favor local suppliers as an economic development strategy. Massachusetts's law denying state procurement contracts to companies doing business with Burma, for example, was overturned in the U.S. courts because they anticipated it would violate the WTO. A Minnesota law providing tax breaks to encourage microbreweries,

Oklahoma's and Texas's laws giving procurement preferences to local businesses hiring Texans and Oklahomans, other states' laws that give preferences to minority-owned firms—all these could be challenged as violating the WTO's so-called nondiscrimination provisions.

The WTO already has an agreement on "trade-related investment measures," called TRIMs. Established in 1994, this deal outlaws all kinds of government regulations designed to ensure that foreign investments contribute to local economic development. In former eras, governments were more powerful than entrepreneurs and able to require certain behaviors of them. Typically, national laws would require investors to hire a certain percentage of local staff, or buy a certain portion of the inputs from local suppliers, or export a certain amount of the production to bring funds into the national economy. Nowadays, the larger companies have consolidated their holdings and acquired enough power to turn it all around—now they can require certain behaviors of governments!

The WTO's General Agreement on Trade in Services (GATS) is still being negotiated, but it promises to give private investors the right to outcompete governments in providing basic services to the public—education, health care, water treatment, waste management, banking, postal services, and on and on—under the rules of National Treatment. A Canadian law firm, for example, has issued a legal opinion finding the GATS could end Canada's preference for Canadian textbooks, Canadian university professors, Canadian financial assistance for

Canadian students, and so on. Similarly, a U.S.-based health maintenance organization (HMO) or any other medical services provider could use the WTO to declare Canada's renowned health care system illegal, because the private firms may not compete for patients. The GATS could also make illegal Canada's laws giving the provinces control over their water supplies, and thus force the provincial governments to allow private companies to take over water management.

Fortunately, campaigners have succeeded in convincing the media that requiring neurotoxins and carcinogens in our gasoline to fulfill NAFTA's Chapter 11 is newsworthy. Public awareness about the WTO's services negotiations, GATS, mounts daily. Activists soundly defeated the Multilateral Agreement on Investment (MAI) proposed in the late 1990s, after several years of dedicated campaigning. It may be that trade negotiators will be forced by civil society to restore limits to the rights of investors—and perhaps even redefine their responsibilities—in favor of public health, the environment, jobs, and local and regional economic development strategies.

But from a corporate point of view, the creation of public guarantees for investors is such a great idea that it keeps popping up. Not only are various elements of investors' rights on the table for the ongoing WTO negotiations, but they also appear in drafts of the proposed Free Trade Area of the Americas (FTAA)—a U.S.-inspired plan to extend NAFTA throughout Latin America—and in innumerable bilateral deals including the U.S.-Chile and U.S.-Singapore agreements.

After all, the biggest global investors are the wealthiest and, arguably, the most powerful people on Earth. And when diplomatic avenues seem blocked, there are other means. As Venezuela's President Hugo Chavez refused to privatize that country's national oil sector, well-financed opposition parties have coordinated huge protests with support from the international business community. And there is always military force with which to pursue powerful interests.

WAR AND WEAPONS

The desire to gain control of the world's oil supply is undoubtedly a motive behind the U.S. attack on and occupation of Iraq, but the thirst for unrivaled global power must also drive President Bush and his cohorts in the White House—evidenced in their actions to divide and conquer a new and strategically unified EU. Meanwhile, vast economic opportunities in the global arms industry continually stimulate the whole dirty business.

It's probably fair to say that defeating terrorism is a relatively minor goal—certainly it was of little interest to the United States before September 11, 2001. Immediately afterward, President Bush's international coalition to defeat terrorism, "wherever it may exist," was promptly backed up by the UN Security Council, which on September 28, 2001 passed Resolution 1373, creating a new international legal obligation to cooperate in preventing terrorism. But not without UN Secretary-

General Kofi Annan pointing out that a number of earlier treaties designed to quell terrorism still needed U.S. ratification—treaties to regulate offshore accounts and other havens for laundering dirty money, to which the United States finally did subscribe in June 2002. (To its credit, Annan's office also put the UN's human rights treaty bodies on alert in the post–September 11 context, to look for possible abuses of force in the guise of combating terrorism.)

The United States is a world superpower, but its leadership has brought about neither universal prosperity nor respect for human rights, and its unilateral style fails to promote international cooperation and peace. Indeed, the United States' refusal to participate in the newly launched International Criminal Court—the perfect instrument for a global response to the attacks of September 11 and dictators like Hussein—typifies the problem.

Yes, if they survive, we need to try Saddam Hussein and Osama bin Laden for their crimes against humanity, but we also must have the power to try world leaders for crimes as well; we need to support the rights of the Israelis and Palestinians equally, to facilitate the end of the Israeli occupation and the emergence of a sovereign Palestinian state; we need to ensure food security and development for the Iraqis, Afghanis, and all peoples; to ensure access to medicines for people living with HIV and other illnesses; and to share resources and the responsibility for global warming and other threats to planetary survival. These international problems require international cooperation, yet militarism—as is true of regional competition over valuable resources, the multiple ongoing civil wars, and the United States' aggressive unilateralism—is more the norm.

In 2001, Carlos Menem was arrested on charges of leading a conspiracy to sell 6,575 tons of weapons and explosives to Croatia and Ecuador during his Argentine presidency. Peru's president, Alberto Fujimori, and spy-chief Vladimiro Montesinos were forced into exile in 2000 for involvement in illegal weapons trading with Colombia's guerilla army. A senior official in the Rwandan government, Theoneste Bagosora, worked with former South African official Ters Ehlers and the government of the Seychelles Islands to bring arms into that war-torn region, channeling funds through a chain of Swiss, French, and Italian banks before being indicted for the murder of UN peacekeepers there. Charles Taylor, Liberia's president, has a bloody record of smuggling weapons to Sierra Leone. Alas, there are plenty of other arms brokers gaining from political influence.

Small arms are big business: about $9 billion worth of handguns and light weapons are traded yearly, according to one estimate. The widening gap between rich and poor is fueling hostilities all over the world, and the lucrative armaments industry is ready to supply both sides. A UN Commission of Inquiry published reports in 1996 and 1998 documenting this lucrative industry and the private dealers who "profit from conflicts, the trade in illicit arms and diamonds, and, not least, on the transport of such illicit merchandise." This commission concluded that the profiteers are "instrumental in facilitating war and armed conflict."

Of course, the gun dealers have fertile ground to work with. Poverty and environmental degradation on the one hand, and utter despair on the other, create near-ideal conditions for the recruitment of guerilla armies. The Andean region writhes with violence and well-organized rebellions. The Fuerzas Armadas Revolucionarias de Colombia, the FARC, consists largely of desperate peasants under siege from the so-called war on drugs that pours billions of U.S. taxpayer dollars into arms and helicopters and toxic herbicides. Aerial fumigation is the weapon of choice against coca farmers, who really have no choice but to produce the plant because it's the only crop that generates a livable income. Antigovernment forces, too, easily attract the rural dispossessed in Peru, where Sendero Luminoso reigns with brutal terror.

In some cases, the combatants have clearly stated political objectives linked to their opposition to the economic institutions driving globalization. Highly organized networks of indigenous peoples in Ecuador successfully took over their government in 2000 in a popular and bloodless coup lasting just one day, and in 2002 they marched en masse against the FTAA, or ALCA, the Spanish-language acronym for the Free Trade Area of the Americas. And it was on the first day of NAFTA, on January 1, 1994, that armed peasants from the Mexican state of Chiapas declared the trade agreement to be "a death sentence for the Indian people of Mexico" and demanded instead "liberty and political democracy," including "clean elections in all levels of the government."

To this day, the indigenous people of Chiapas and their Zapatista army sustain control of large areas of the region despite numerous attempts by the federal army to defeat them. The administration of President Vicente Fox (formerly of Coca-Cola) has been willing to engage with the Zapatistas in political negotiations—but a breakthrough has yet to emerge.

The Zapatistas' renowned spokesperson, Subcomandante Marcos, explained their revolt as a response to unfair terms of trade. "Chiapas loses blood through many veins," he wrote in a memo circulated globally via the Internet:

> ...through oil and gas ducts, electric lines, train cars, bank accounts, trucks and vans, boats and planes...petroleum, electric energy, cattle money, coffee, banana, honey, corn, cacao, tobacco, sugar, soy, melon, sorghum, mamey, mango, tamarind, avocado...and Chiapan blood flows...towards different parts of the world: the United States, Canada, Holland, Germany, Italy, Japan...A handful of businesses, one of which is the state of Mexico, take all the wealth out of Chiapas leaving behind in exchange their mortal and pestilent track...ecological destruction, agricultural scraps, hyperinflation, alcoholism, prostitution and poverty.

Similar stories can be told about Angola, the Congo, Kosovo and Serbia, Russia and Chechnya, Israel and Palestine, India and Pakistan, Ethiopia and Eritrea, Sudan, Somalia, Algeria, and Afghanistan—the list goes on and on. Tribal and ethnic disputes, religious fundamentalism, military coups, egomaniacal power plays, ideological supremacy, cultural intractability, land and resource grabs, Mafia-style gangsterism, Cold War leftovers—the historical circumstances vary enormously, but in each case, the fighting can be traced to perceived injustice, deprivation, and political oppression by dominating interests.

The post–Cold War, neoliberal period of free trade has done nothing to alleviate the conflicts. To the contrary, President Bush and his military buddies Cheney and Rumsfeld are pursuing the "war on terror" in multiple countries. Afghanistan, North Korea, the Philippines, Sudan, Somalia, Iran, and other countries have all been mentioned as possible havens for terrorists, however vaguely linked to al-Qaeda. Antiterrorism rhetoric has been invoked to escalate U.S. involvement in Iraq and in Colombia's civil war. The Bush administration's $2.1 trillion budget for 2002–03 includes $356 billion for the military, an increase of 11 percent over the previous year and more than 14 percent above Cold War spending levels! Large chunks of these taxpayer dollars will flow to private defense contractors.

Other industrialized powers, too, partake of the arms industry bonanza: As a whole, the G-8 countries account for 75 percent of the world's annual $800 billion military expenditure, 87 percent of the $40 billion trade in weapons, and 98 percent of the 31,000 nuclear weapons in the world. Clearly there are mercenary and political motives on top of any humanitarian objectives.

The Women's International League for Peace and Freedom and the Arms Trade Resource Center have identified "the dirtiest dozen" partners in the major weapons business—many of them the same contractors who have benefited from contracts with the World Bank over the years. Among them:

- ➤ IBM manufactures and sells supercomputers for designing nuclear weapons and missiles, with sales in India, Russia and China.

- ➤ Bechtel Corporation conducts nuclear experiments at the Nevada test site, which it manages, and recently it helped found the Committee for the Liberation of Iraq.

- ➤ Boeing is the prime contractor for the National Missile Defense system.

- ➤ Alliant is the largest supplier of all munitions to the U.S. Department of Defense.

- ➤ General Dynamics is the U.S. Navy's leading supplier of combat vessels, including nuclear submarines.

- ➤ Siemens sells electronic communication systems and plutonium to the military, while constructing and servicing nuclear power plants.

➤ About half of the nuclear power plants in the world, and more than half in the United States, are operated with Westinghouse technology, now owned by British Nuclear Fuels (BNFL), which buys uranium and manages its processing into fuel.

➤ Lockheed Martin is the world's largest weapons contractor, acquiring, along with Boeing, TRW, and Raytheon, two thirds of all Pentagon contracts.

➤ British Aerospace Electronics (BAE) is the biggest arms-producing company in the world, since acquiring Lockheed Martin's Aerospace Electronics Systems.

President Bush's recent nuclear pact with Russia's President Putin undercuts the earlier Nuclear Non-Proliferation Treaty (NPT). The new pact calls for reductions in both countries' long-range nuclear arsenals but does not require their destruction; either government can redeploy them at any time under the terms of the new deal. The pact does not address short-range and tactical nuclear weapons, and the U.S. recently developed the "bunker buster," which they've coined the "Mother of All Bombs" (MOAB). In short, the Bush administration has sparked a whole new arms race, encouraging Russia as well as China, India, Pakistan, and Israel to further develop their own nuclear weapons of mass destruction.

In addition, the Bush administration's "Son of Star Wars" missile defense strategy violates the Anti-Ballistic Missile Treaty (ABM). Less well reported in the media than Saddam Hussein's biological and chemical weapons factories is the United States' continued research and development of weapons banned under the Chemical Weapons Convention (CWC) and Biological and Toxin Weapons Conventions (BTWC). Amongst the newest inventions in the U.S. experimental arsenal are neurological gases that, more effectively than tear gas and pepper spray, will tranquilize protesters.

The 1972 BTWC bans the development, production, and stockpiling of bacteriological and toxic agents intended for hostile purposes. So far, 144 countries—including the United States—have ratified the BTWC and talks were progressing on a Verification Protocol. But on July 25 2002, President Bush pulled the United States out of the verification negotiations, suggesting that UN weapons inspectors might conduct industrial espionage. Then in November, as public fears over anthrax grew, he suddenly announced a seven-point plan to strengthen the treaty, calling for national criminal laws against violators and UN inspections of countries suspected of using biological weapons and places with suspicious disease outbreaks. But this latest plan still leaves out regular surprise international inspections of all bioweapons research facilities.

Nearly all the technology needed to develop offensive biological warfare can also be used for legitimate medical and biological research, and can even be conducted in the same laboratory. Modern breakthroughs in biotechnology have boosted the development of new highly sophisticated and dangerous biological weapons. And the United States is the primary political and financial force behind them. Since 1998, the research and field testing of bioweapons have been conducted with U.S. encouragement and financial support through the UN Drug Control Program (UNDCP). An international campaign aimed at gaining support for this program persuaded the United Kingdom to provide a biological war-on-drugs program.

Among the contemporary developments, the use of bioweapons to kill drug-producing crops of coca, opium, and marijuana in Asia and South America has provoked controversy. These anticrop weapons also affect wild plants and agriculture in fragile and diverse ecosystems, where they can self-replicate indefinitely, as well as endanger human health. Illicit crop workers in Asia and Latin America are mostly poor peasants whose families live in drug-producing areas. Children play in narcotic-producing fields and are exposed to the agents, whether biological or chemical, used in the war against drugs. Thousands of people have been treated for chemical poisoning in drug-affected areas in Colombia, where a U.S.-sponsored program fumigates illicit crops. Then in November 2000, after tumultuous campaigning led by civic leaders from the Andean region, with the support of concerned people worldwide, the UNDCP withdrew its support of plans to use biological agents against the coca shrub in Colombia and the Andean region. Nongovernmental organizations concerned with the proliferation of biological weapons welcomed the UN decision; however, they warned that antidrug biological weapons programs are still active in Asia and the United States.

Nearly 120 wars have been fought since the end of World War II, the "war to end all wars." More than 25 million people have been killed since then and an additional 75 million injured—nearly as many casualties as in World War II itself. And more and more of the victims are noncombatants. In the last decade, some 4 million civilians have died as victims of conflict, and nearly 40 million people have been displaced from their home territories by these wars. The number of Iraqis killed, maimed, or injured by America's attack may never be fully and accurately counted.

As time passes, September 11 becomes part of the awful historical record of people killing other people. And we are still left with the question: What can we do about it?

Part IV

CITIZEN ACTION

The beginning of the twenty-first century may be remembered by historians as an era of popular unrest: terrible acts of repression by local police trained by private companies with direct ties to various national security forces, massive demonstrations by a newly conceived "global civil society," and the repeal of civil rights. In addition to this spectacular phase of resistance and containment, marked by national legal reforms and the strengthening of supranational institutional authority, historians may also record truly revolutionary developments in international diplomatic procedures that beckon toward democratic possibilities at the global level.

ANTIGLOBALIZATION PROTESTS

"We are writing the Constitution of a single global economy," announced Renato Ruggiero, then head of the WTO, in an October 1996 speech to the UN Conference on Trade and Development. Afterward he denied saying so. In Seattle three years later, it became obvious why he'd tried to repress the comment: the WTO would be the last place in the world you'd want to plant your flag claiming global governance—that is, if you wanted your plan to work.

The so-called antiglobalization campaign certainly preceded the 1999 Battle of Seattle, growing steadily stronger over the past two or three decades in opposition to the social injustices and environmental policies of international economic institutions. The removal of dictators by popular forces in a dozen or more countries, human-rights campaigns against debt, and World Bank projects such as the Narmada River Dams characterized the early period of today's movement. So, too, resistance to U.S. military invasions in Asia and Latin America during the 1980s contributed to the development of transnational citizen action. When activists plunged through the Berlin Wall, relations opened not just between Eastern and Western Europe but also among civil societies worldwide.

During the NAFTA campaign in the early nineties, trinational gatherings of autoworkers, clothing workers, communications workers, dairy farmers, and corn producers were similarly galvanized, brainstorming sectoral as well as continental strategies to defend wages, the right to organize, rural communities, and fair trade. Along with environmentalists and other civil society groups, they focused on NAFTA's likely impacts on employment, housing, pollution, and health in the U.S.-Mexican border region.

Regional trade negotiations between the United States and Asia-Pacific countries and between Europe and its former colonies in the African, Caribbean, and Pacific regions geared up simultaneously, and by the mid-1990s, all these networks began to focus on the WTO.

Farmer, labor, environmental, and consumer groups actively fought the Uruguay round of trade negotiations with the image of "GATT-zilla" overwhelming the towers of national democracy. Labor and environmental issues are probably the hottest debates, uniting the "Turtles-to-Teamsters" coalition at the Third WTO Ministerial meeting in Seattle and embracing the challenge of investors' rights—the corporate attack on public sector services as well as the environment.

Enraged by the use of tear –gas—ostensibly in response to a small group of vandals—and the otherwise exceptionally brutal treatment by the Seattle police of all fifty thousand demonstrators assembled there, the new generation of youthful antiglobalization protesters next gathered in Washington, D.C. in April 2000, where the World Bank and IMF were meeting. From there they went to Prague for a meeting of the G-8. Also that year, the nominating conventions of both the Republican and Democratic Parties in the United States were plagued with protests, as were the conventions of several industry groups, particularly the biotechnology industry.

Then on to Quebec City in April 2001, where thirty-four out of thirty-five governments in the Western hemisphere (all except Cuba) began negotiating the FTAA. Again, some fifty thousand activists, led by trade unions with lots of support from all the other sectors of civil society, protested the United States' neocolonial corporate agenda for the hemisphere, and, again, the police reacted with extreme measures including tear gas, fire hoses, arrests, and beatings. In June 2001, protesters at a G-8 meeting in Genoa were attacked by the Italian police with rubber bullets and one was killed.

Later in 2001, the Fourth WTO Ministerial was held in Doha, Qatar, in the United Arab Emirates, a place so remote and controlled that officials would not have to deal with huge angry crowds. While smaller in numbers, representatives of the major public interest groups— labor, environmental, farmer, consumer, and so on— were joined by AIDS activists to demand the WTO affirm the intellectual property rules permitting countries to manufacture or import generic drugs instead of paying extra for the patented name brands. Also in Doha, farm organizations brought a proposal that could lead to waivers of some of the worst WTO rules hurting small-scale farms and rural communities, and it was adopted by developing country governments.

While these global campaigns languish in WTO negotiations on implementation, they are backed by national campaigns to reinforce or attack each government's position in the international negotiations. With strong national capacity, regional and international strategies become more feasible. Increasingly, these well-organized national efforts are seen as the key to global achievements. A few recent accomplishments at the national level promise much wider implications internationally:

➤ Advocates for affordable AIDS drugs in South Africa defeated a patent-infringement lawsuit filed by nineteen pharmaceutical companies. Buoyed by this victory, Brazilians then beat back a U.S. threat to use the WTO's dispute system to challenge their national health policy providing free and low-cost AIDS drugs to people in need, regardless of the patents.

➤ Farmers in India organized a "Seed Satyagraha"—a campaign of nonviolent civil disobedience modeled on Ghandi's "Salt Satyagraha" of 1930 that led to India's independence from the British—declaring their noncooperation with proposed new patent laws covering seeds and other genetic resources.

➤ In Ethiopia, model legislation was drafted that is now being promoted throughout the continent by the African Union (formerly the Organization for African Unity) to protect the rights of indigenous peoples and local communities to their knowledge and natural resources under national laws.

➤ Citizens in Cochabamba, Bolivia, successfully defeated the privatization of their water supply by the Bechtel Corporation. Similar campaigns to defend community access and public control of freshwater are under way in Ghana, Pakistan, Canada, and many other countries.

But this describes only the current generation of international campaigners. So, too, the anticolonialist era marked by new democracies emerging from Spanish, British, French, and Portuguese domination should be considered part of this history. And certainly the antislavery and women's suffrage movements presaged those of today. In fact, anti-imperialism dates back at least to the Greek and Roman empires.

The 1999 Battle of Seattle marks an exceptional moment in history, however, for numerous reasons. For one thing, the protesters were victorious: the WTO meeting ended abruptly and in absolute official failure. For another, and probably most important, it was the Caribbean, African, Asian, and some Latin American governments that decisively pulled the plug, opening a new era of solidarity and collaboration between global civil society and these governments. Three, the Seattle police made a huge mistake in allowing the violence to escalate. As a result, virtually every U.S. citizen across the country was shocked by the revealing images on their television screens. And four, the protesters were diverse—trade unionists, environmental and consumer advocates, indigenous peoples, farmers, antiwar advocates, and ordinary concerned citizens were all in attendance—and included large numbers of informed and organized young people, whose commitment to building broader awareness of the problems of globalization persists.

The unity behind this diversity of interests is stunning. Despite their differing motivations, all of these constituencies feel the impact of decisions being made at the international level, decisions in which they, the public, have no say. Democracy is at stake. Now, the old slogan "No justice, no peace!" again throbs in the air as police, armed in full battle gear, attack protesters with tear gas and rubber bullets in attempt to quell the crowds.

PRO-JUSTICE GLOBALISM

Somehow, it is encouraging to realize that the brutal upping of the stakes by government security forces is in response to significant successes by civil society. The so-called antiglobalization movement—which despite the rubric is not antiglobalization at all, but determinedly pro–global justice—collectively negotiated the terrain of international diplomacy to win real victories:

> ➤ In 1994, a small number of activists formed a coalition, convinced a few key governments, lobbied strategically, and just three years later a treaty banning land mines was born. The rapidity of this negotiation alone is astounding, but so is the unique way in which the nongovernmental International Campaign to Ban Landmines initiated the project and carried it through—without the support of the world's most powerful governments.

> ➤ The Jubilee 2000 network, building upon decades of work by others, convinced the IMF, World Bank, and a number of govern-

ments to cancel nearly $100 billion of the debt owed by heavily indebted poor countries. The network continues to demand greater cancellation, challenging the very legitimacy of the loans' terms in the first place.

➤ In 2001, nongovernmental groups formed an alliance with a team of legal experts to create the Model Convention on Arms Brokering, a document aimed at regulating the illicit global trade in small weapons.

➤ It was the proposals of nongovernmental organizations that in July 2002, despite U.S. opposition, broke through the intransigence of governments to at last establish the International Criminal Court—a proposal that had languished in diplomatic limbo since the Holocaust.

Each of these success stories is rooted in the shared commitment of citizens from many countries to work together to build a coalition strong enough to persuade their governments to take official action. Each victory has depended upon an international group of well-connected activists who are also expert in their fields and sophisticated enough to weld the popular thirst for justice with several governments' strategic interests. But this sophistication is not cynical or self-promoting; it is instead derived from experience, commitment, and a sharp sense of the global public interest.

A decade ago, when the UN celebrated the twentieth anniversary of its first environmental negotiations in Stockholm, the Earth Summit of 1992 became its largest gathering of civil society groups ever. Some fifty thousand activists representing organizations from all over the world came together in Rio de Janeiro to show their support for new international environmental laws. Thousands of these groups spent the week on Rio's Flamingo Beach drafting forty-two "treaties" of their own—a series of documents precisely defining their commitment to work with their own communities and national governments, as well as globally, to reorganize values, priorities, and institutions toward achieving sustainable development. The prescriptions were distinct for each of the forty-two sectors—ranging from water to land; from agriculture to labor; from business, to trade, to finance; and so on. And they were quite different from the official treaties that guide international environmental policy to this day, those simultaneously produced across town by governments cloistered behind security gates guarded by Brazilian soldiers and Rio de Janeiro's well-armed police. But among all these civil society treaties, virtually all shared a commitment to participatory democracy and the engagement of local communities.

Then, ten years later, twice as many—some hundred thousand activists—gathered in Porto Alegre, Brazil, for the annual pro–global justice celebration at the World Social Forum. It is always remarkable to discover at such gatherings the degree to which common values and visions of the future are shared by ordinary people from everywhere, no matter their country or culture, whether or not they have ever participated in an international political event before.

Nonetheless, reorganizing the way in which the world works so as to achieve global health and justice is a massive project that will require more than big demonstrations or new international treaties. To seriously address global warming, for example, will require not only restructuring of the powerful transnational energy sector. It will also require changes in the behavior of every one of us on a day-to-day basis. It is not enough for us to recycle in our homes while driving gas-guzzlers, nor would it be enough if every citizen bought the most fuel-efficient automobile in the marketplace. If and when a future U.S. government signs and ratifies the Kyoto Protocol to the UN Framework Convention on Climate Change, it will still take the combined efforts of citizen action groups across the country—and in other countries—to monitor local industries and report noncompliance; to demand the procurement of alternative-fuel vehicles for their local and state and national governments' automobile fleets; to build new housing projects powered by wind and geothermal heat exchangers; to work with farm groups and support ethanol and other biofuels; to buy food from nearby farming communities; and to coordinate other forms of rural-urban exchange.

Global policies can be a stimulus for reform, but any global solution requires widespread local support and most require local implementation. The role of individuals in defining a local vision, organizing committees to generate public support, building the political capacity to engage local governments, and ensuring equitable tax and financing mechanisms to pay for implementation is key. So, too, is restructuring the economy so that local consumers procure from local producers via local distributors, bypassing the corporate chains.

Linking such local initiatives—on both the policy level and the practical level—across the country and throughout the planet is how pro–global justice activists imagine achieving the dream of international economic and political democracy.

DEMOCRACY

Here in the United States, we tend to associate the term "democracy" with elections. To be sure, the right to participate in the selection of our political leaders is fundamental, but so are freedom of speech, freedom of movement, and freedom of association. These freedoms are what makes for a healthy civil society—a culture bubbling with neighborhood associations and parent-teacher associations, labor unions and trade associations, cultural groups, recreation clubs, consumer and environmentalist lobbies, teen clubs and ethnic dancing clubs, chapters of the NAACP and the Urban League, Latinos Unidos, Asian business associations, and every other voluntary grouping you might imagine. The flourishing of such citizens' organizations is probably the real hallmark of a democracy—even where elections can be rigged and stolen.

The peaceful resolution of disputes between free and independent individuals or between different associations of people is also fundamental. And, as is true of the formation of civil society groups, this process, too, is easier within a close-knit community than across international borders. It's hard enough for neighbors arguing over a backyard fence to settle their gripes, let alone 5 billion people speaking thousands of different languages on seven continents. So the bigger the universe of stakeholders, the greater the dependence upon representative leadership instead of direct participation—and the greater the likelihood of exclusion from decision-making processes.

At the most local level, say, a town meeting to decide whether to build a new school, democracy can work pretty well. Word gets around, people discuss it for weeks at the coffee shop and grocery store, meetings get organized, and people speak up. Passions can grow strong on multiple sides of an issue, but eventually it seems clear that a majority favors one decision or another.

At a more regional level, perhaps the county or state or province will have to decide whether to help finance new schools. Maybe a couple people from the first town car-pool to the big city to visit with their elected officials, bring along a petition signed by hundreds of community members in favor of schools, and even testify in front of some microphones. Probably the decision won't get made that same day; more likely, a vote will be held much later forcing choices within a bigger budget package—schools or sewers? Or maybe it's a matter of a new highway versus subsidies for a shopping center. Either way, the townspeople will read about it in the newspapers.

At the national level, a newly elected president (or prime minister) might try to keep a campaign promise to build new schools and in turn get a lot of positive media coverage about it—at first. Over many months, other issues, maybe taxes or a war, take over. The national Congress(or Parliament), more accessible to their constituents than the president, remind the president and each other from time to time that most voters back home want their kids to get a good education, yet they know others care more about lower taxes. Most of their constituency never visits their offices nor even writes a letter, but they get plenty of visits from lobbyists promoting highways and subsidies for business. In fact, the lobbyists even give them money (legally!) to promote their interests. At the end of the year, the congressional representatives go home to campaign for their reelection and explain that they tried to support schools but they were outvoted. The president, meanwhile, collects millions of dollars in campaign contributions from every conceivable lobbyist and promises to build new schools next year.

At the global level—wow! Typically, the president (or some other head of state) appoints prominent, experienced international experts—say, a former military officer, an executive from industry, a retired lobbyist, or maybe a former banker—to serve the nation in various offices handling foreign affairs. The citizens probably have never heard of these people until (and if) their appointments are announced in the newspapers. And all too often, the public is unaware of the international policies they will be negotiating on their behalf. No hearings are held, no ballot initiatives are offered, no plebiscite is undertaken, and there is virtually no way to engage in the national decision-making process that directs foreign policy.

But there could be. It could become law that every international negotiation becomes the subject of a national policy debate; the form of this debate could well be structured to ensure participation at the local level. Here in the United States, we could require the broadcasting networks to air the full range of opinions in exchange for their access to the nation's airwaves. We could establish a role for local, state, and even regional organizations in formulating a national mandate. For example, the National Association of Mayors, the fifty states' legislative assemblies, the states' attorneys general, and the National Governors Association might all be asked their views and perhaps even be entitled to some percentage in the ultimate decision-making formula, alongside Congress and the White House.

But does greater democracy necessarily bring about a more just society? Certainly there are many cases in which popular views are not just—racism comes to mind. And by definition, a minority group can be excluded from a democratic majority. On the other hand, many civil wars are being fought today to overcome political domination by a powerful minority. In the parliamentary system practiced in Europe and many other countries around the world, politicians wishing to govern must develop working coalitions amongst minor political parties, each with diverse priorities, sufficient to attain a democratic majority; and then leaders must sustain the coalition to stay in power. In the United States' electoral system, however, the two dominant parties have a monopoly on power—a monopoly so unpopular that less than 40 percent of eligible voters even bothered to vote in the presidential election taken by George W. Bush amid charges of electoral fraud. And together, the two parties have established procedures making it extremely difficult for any third party to gain the foothold necessary to challenge their control.

Ralph Nader, the anticorporate, pro–global justice consumer advocate who scraped together 5 percent of the national vote in the presidential election of 2000, thus attaining official third-party status for the U.S. Green Party, likens the Democrats and Republicans to "Tweedledum and Tweedledee." Of course, there are many votes in our Congress reflecting fierce bipartisan differences, but most reform proposals merely skim the surface of an issue, leaving corporate power unscathed. And ironically, the fiercest of differences result in watered-down compromise or even stalemates! The debate over how to provide affordable drugs in the 2002 congressional session resulted in no new legislation at all, because the two parties would not find a compromise between their proposals, both of which would have subsidized the pharmaceutical companies with taxpayer dollars, albeit to varying degrees.

A more democratic approach to international policy making in the United States necessitates the creation of political space for new and alternative views to be aired as broadly as those of the major parties and their candidates, and a balance between corporate influence and the public interest. We could require that industry executives retire for a period of time before they can represent the public in governmental matters. Likewise, there could be a time lapse required before high-level politicians and civil servants may accept executive jobs within those industries they may have supported or regulated. And it could be made absolutely illegal to accept campaign contributions, gifts, or other veiled bribery from corporations.

CITIZEN SCIENCE

We might want to democratize how decisions get made in the pursuit of scientific knowledge too. Indeed, the privatization of science, like the privatization of other resources, represents a critical threat to human and ecological health, public welfare, and justice.

As research and development has become increasingly expensive, our government and the public universities have found it easier to raise money from the private sector than from taxpayers. On many campuses, new labs with the best equipment and bright new architecture can only be built with the support of major companies—and the knowledge gleaned benefits their bottom lines, particularly when they can control the commercial application of the new knowledge with a patent. Even publicly funded research and the associated patent rights held by a public university are often licensed to private developers for commercial application. Most ironic, the private sector gives back, in the form of grants to universities, just a fraction of what it is exempted in taxes.

As a result, more and more research is skewed away from the public interest, with gigantic investments, for example, going into genetically engineered seeds that cannot reproduce (the infamous "Terminator" technology) or crops resistant to Monsanto's Roundup Ready herbicide, instead of the treatment of malaria or other tropical diseases that kill hundreds of millions of the world's poor every year. Furthermore, in the drive to be first in line at the patent office, researchers now tend to horde their findings, often as a condition of their employment, slowing down the ultimate discovery of a new vaccine or some other knowledge valuable to all humanity.

While research is increasingly biased toward generating returns for commercial interests, a great deal of valuable traditional knowledge is also being lost to humanity. The expertise of farmers managing the interactions of specific varieties of seed with specific soil conditions amid specific insect and bacteriological populations and specific climatalogical circumstances cannot be exchanged for a laboratory-tested commercial generally distributed variety. Nor can the knowledge of traditional healers and shamans be replicated by a doctor with a pill, despite the fact that most of the active ingredients in pharmaceutical drugs derive from a plant or other biological resource.

"Technology transfer" has been deemed one of the goals of international cooperation for development, yet it is mostly perceived as a matter of transferring high-tech types of knowledge from the industrialized world to the less developed countries. On the one hand, this is a short-sighted approach that could be greatly enhanced by pursuing a two-way exchange of traditional know-how and innovative practices. On the other hand, there's a need to examine just how the encroachment of high-tech science may erode alternative knowledge systems. When technology transfer is achieved by force, rather than as a result of mutual understanding and a shared research agenda, the results can be not merely antidemocratic but socially and ecologically destructive.

Just such a forceful imposition of technology is promoted by the WTO agreement through obligatory patent protection measures in its TRIPS agreement. When indigenous peoples and traditional communities objected, citing the Convention on Biological Diversity's mandate to "respect, preserve and maintain knowledge, innovations and practices of indigenous and local communities in biodiversity conservation," a major diplomatic debate ensued to reconcile these two international treaties. At the center of the debate is a UN agency, the World Intellectual Property Organization (WIPO), whose charge has shifted as a result of the conflict. Formerly, it served as an archive or clearinghouse for all the intellectual property agreements worldwide; since the TRIPS agreement was enacted, WIPO has moved into providing "technical assistance" to assist governments in their implementation of the TRIPS rules. Indigenous peoples and farming groups have criticized WIPO for this shift, while they simultaneously seek to limit and roll back the TRIPS agreement itself, or at least achieve acknowledgment within the WTO that the Convention on Biological Diversity must also be implemented.

Within the UN Food and Agriculture Organization, too, diplomats are meeting with farm groups to settle the "apparent conflicts" identified by the UN's Office of the High Commissioner for Human Rights between TRIPS and farmers' rights to save, use, exchange, and sell farm-saved seed. A new international treaty on plant genetic resources for food and agriculture has defined farmers' rights as a matter of national responsibility, while creating a multilateral system to ensure that the exchange of seeds and other reproductive material still in the public domain will not be limited by patents and other intellectual property rights.

In many communities, especially where the erosion of knowledge and the environment is problematic, participatory projects to engage neighbors in the protection of seeds, plants, and ecosystems as well as agricultural and medicinal know-how have been launched. Less common, but equally needed, are projects to define, finance, and pursue an agenda for research –and development based upon the community's needs and resources. There is a grave need for public support and public control of our government's research-and-development agenda. Indeed, private control of any public resource is inherently anti-democratic and unjust. Yet the presence of injustice is not only a moral issue. It is of serious consequence for the orderly running of a nation: injustice breeds insecurity, insecurity breeds violence.

Part V

WHAT IS POSSIBLE?

"Sustainable development is *the* peace policy." That's how the head of the UN Environment Program, Klaus Topfer, once Germany's environment minister, has put it.

Acknowledging a certain lack of precision, many pro–global justice campaigners also use the term "sustainable development" in describing the alternative to the devastating model of development now unfolding. Spearheaded by environmentalists who see the resources of the planet depleting faster than they can be regenerated, the call for a "sustainable" model has come to embrace economic and social health and resilience as well. Many activists consider this triad—economic, ecological, and social sustainability—to be the foundation of the future, while another threesome—governments, the private sector, and civil society—form the pillars that must share the weight of its construction.

While many campaigns are necessarily based on responding to the multiple and complex crises facing people and the planet, there is a growing awareness of the need for practical proposals for achieving long-term sustainability. Gradually, an agenda for a peaceful, just, democratic, and sustainable reorganization of the global governance framework is taking shape. Here are some key elements of a growing consensus:

➤ *Market fundamentalism is not working.* As deregulation of financial and trade markets increases, poverty, inequality, and incidences of violence increase as well. In 2001, then UN High Commissioner for Human Rights Mary Robinson called globalization in general, and the WTO in particular, "a nightmare for the poor, especially the developing countries in the South," and pointed out "apparent conflicts" between the WTO's approach to agriculture, intellectual property rights, and services on the one hand, and the UN human rights laws on the other.

➤ *Meeting the basic needs of humanity is a nonnegotiable demand.* Those with the least resources and privilege are the greatest victims of the rapidly globalizing model of development. Within nations, too, the poorest are excluded from society's decision-making processes. As the authors of "Reimagining the Future," a brilliant report on global-governance reform sponsored by several Western Pacific groups, explain, "Given that inequalities of wealth and income lead to unequal access to knowledge and influence, democratizing governance both requires and promotes distributive justice."

➤ *The public sphere must be protected, and within it human needs and human rights, labor rights, and cultural and ecological integrity.* The exploitation of people and nature is rampant. The private sector has found clever mechanisms to privatize labor, genes, and water and is working on ways to buy and sell air and traditional knowledge. Yolanda Kakabadse, head of the International Union for the Conservation of Nature (IUCN) and former minister of the environment for Ecuador, put it this way: "Is the Earth a market?...Or a planet?"

➤ *Corporate and elite power must be regulated.* The drive for profitability in the present system of corporate accounts overwhelms the moral drive of even the most sincere executive, while the privileges and temptations that come with great wealth build a slippery slope down which most slide pretty fast. Marjorie Kelly, publisher of the journal *Business Ethics*, compares corporate executives to the lords and dukes and viscounts of imperial aristocracies. Just as the nobility viewed all other humans as commoners to be ignored, today's executives, she points out, see employees as "expenses to be cut...A primary bias built into financial statements is the notion that stockholders are to be paid as much as possible, whereas employees are to be paid as little as possible." And the executive doing so the best gets to be king.

➤ *Democratic systems of justice must be accessible to everyone in global decision making.* Better democratization of our national governments is essential but not enough. Even outside formal government structures, organized associations of individuals voicing their views and pursuing their interests within their communities and across national boundaries contribute substantially to the democratic formulation of decisions. Former UN Secretary-General Boutros Boutros-Ghali listed necessary components of meeting the challenge of "democracy beyond borders": increased participation for regional organizations, more involvement for parliamentarians and local authorities, greater participation of civil society as well as business and industry, and a role for the media. In short, mechanisms of communication, representation, and accountability must reach back and forth from remote villages to those who will govern the corporate kings.

PROPOSALS FOR CHANGE

Attend any gathering of pro–global justice activists discussing the way forward and the above five elements of an emerging consensus will resonate loud and clear. Proposals abound, rich with detail. Equally rich debates can be heard, as civil society groups in every country consider their impacts locally and nationally, and articulate significantly nuanced approaches for implementation in their specific context. Organizing based on many of these proposals is also active and strengthening—within and across national borders.

Below I summarize just a few of the more prevalent ideas, according to the five elements described above—hopefully in a way that engages more of us in the work of constructing a more democratic approach to global governance.

1. Managing Markets

Let's start by digging out some fifty-year-old documents.

The Havana Charter of 1948 laid out plans for an "International Trade Organization"—one that would have been very different than the WTO we know today. This ITO was designed to achieve full employment, rising incomes, and improved standards of living throughout the world. It even recognized the ILO formed in 1919. The Havana Charter set out clear policies for the ITO to administer: supporting industrial stability and fair labor standards as essential to trade expansion; defending protectionism to promote economic development; limiting subsidies so as to fairly allocate world markets; managing supplies as well as prices through negotiated commodity agreements; and prohibiting monopolies or cartels, whether public or private. Indeed, these provisions are consistent with many of today's proposals to reform the WTO!

Some of the provisions of the original GATT deserve implementation today too. Article VI of the GATT, for example, defines and condemns "dumping"—that is, the export of goods at prices below the cost of production. Article XI permits governments to adopt domestic supply management, even allowing restrictions on imports that might favor domestic producers, in order to control production levels, avoid the temptation to dump surpluses, and to relieve food insecurity. These old rules ought to be enforced, and officially reaffirmed if necessary, especially in relation to agriculture.

Alongside managing production and trade in foodstuffs and other essential goods, the global exchange of money needs active management to meet public goals. Like the original ITO and the ILO, the original purposes of the IMF—monetary stabilization through short-term lending and a universal currency—are as valid as ever, as are those of the World Bank in providing low-cost loans to finance development projects where private investors won't go. Some of John Maynard Keynes's proposals that were not accepted back then deserve reconsideration today—including the creation of a universal clearing-house with a global currency in reserve that has the capacity to simultaneously clear the monetary deficits and surpluses of each country and enhance global stability. Some thinkers have proposed greater diversification of the currencies held in national reserves, perhaps with the strongest currency in each region (and certainly with euros), so there is less dependence on the dollar. But why not adopt those obscure "special drawing rights" of the IMF as a universal "hard" currency for use between all the national banks?

Balancing supply and demand is the most effective way to stabilize prices, manage inflation, and smooth out the economy—whether we're talking about dollars and pesos and yen, oil and gas, tin and tungsten, coffee and cotton, or corn and rice and wheat. The key mechanism is a system of reserves that can be released in times of market shortages and stored up in times of surplus. But under trade and financial deregulation, national governments have been forced to give up their rights to manage supply and demand and other aspects of their economies. National controls should be reinstated, linked by regional systems of local reserves coordinated to ensure global stability. Furthermore, the link between real commodity values and real currency values needs to be reestablished. Perhaps a currency exchange rate pegged to each country's or each region's reserve of staple food—is that not the most reliable source of real value to a society?

Other essentials, especially water, similarly deserve public management. Consistent with the recent decision of the UN Committee on Economic, Social, and Cultural Rights declaring the human right to water, public authorities bear the responsibility to ensure supplies and fair distribution to meet demand. Some even argue that larger-scale uses should be considered "abuse," charged prohibitively expensive rates, or even deemed illegal backed with criminal sanctions. Certain nonessential goods, diamonds and weapons, for example, might also deserve to be severely regulated. Taxes may be one way of doing so.

Maybe it is time to set up a global taxing authority based on the principles of taxing "public bads" and "tax broadly, spend closely." In other words, a globally coordinated supply of tax revenues levied on the wealthiest private traders and distributed via regional networks of local authorities could prioritize the neediest for the most urgent public investment. The Tobin Tax, for example, named after the winner of the 1981 Nobel Prize for economics, Sir James Tobin, is a popular proposal nowadays that would levy a tiny tariff on every transaction in the currency exchange markets. Not only would such a tax inhibit the flow of hot money, it would also generate billions of dollars for whatever purposes our global taxing authority might designate. Other possible sources of justly derived international tax revenues include airline tickets, commodity grains, oil, and scarce minerals.

A few other prominent proposals to reregulate trade and financial flows worth mentioning include:

> eliminating all investors' rights schemes returning the authority to our national governments;

➤ rescinding the "trade-related" agreements on intellectual property and investment measures, restoring flexibility in the use of these tools for national development;

➤ creating stringent accounting and auditing standards applicable everywhere and enforceable through criminal sanctions; and

➤ eliminating offshore tax havens.

Above all, we need tough criminal sanctions for the sex trade and other trafficking in human beings, while giving the victims of these industries alternative economic options.

This is the overall message here: markets need to be managed appropriately. Some markets should be outlawed. Some should be supported. Some need governance globally, some need local control, and some should be decentralized but linked regionally. In some cases, say, agricultural production, supply management is essential; in other cases, capital flight, for example, demand must be managed. Some degree of governmental regulation is necessary to direct the market system toward specific public goals.

2. Poverty Alleviation and Development

While regulated markets and the management of supply and demand are primary tools of development, most lists of proposals for immediate poverty alleviation rank debt cancellation and increased foreign aid near the top.

Restructuring economic priorities, the financial system, and, indeed, the whole "model" of development are longer-term but absolutely essential next steps.

Ever since the Baker and Brady plans for debt relief, creditors have shown a growing willingness to write off portions of what is owed them, with the Heavily Indebted Poor Countries Initiative the latest attempt by the banks to recoup even modest sums from virtually insolvent economies. When Argentina defaulted on its debt, it suddenly became time to address the accumulating financial problems of the less impoverished nations too.

Both the IMF and Jubilee 2000, the transnational civil society campaign for debt cancellation, have proposed handling the insolvency of countries similar to the way corporate bankruptcies are handled in the United States. But not surprisingly, there are significant differences in the details of their proposals. Jubilee would create an ad hoc neutral panel under UN auspices to evaluate countries' requests for protection from creditors, while the IMF would retain this authority for itself. The IMF would make bankruptcy protection for a country conditional on implementing the usual structural adjustment program, while Jubilee suggests a process for citizens, civil society organizations, local governments, and the parliaments of the debtor country to determine the conditions, emphasizing that under no circumstances may they override fundamental human rights as defined by the UN.

There are also calls for the total cancellation of all debt incurred under duress of structural adjustment or military dictatorships; write-offs for all but the original principal value or the lowest value that can be bought in secondary and tertiary markets; and "swaps" that would exchange payments for investments in the creation of nature preserves, for example, or investments in immunization programs for children or other spending on development priorities.

Many civil society groups argue that, in fact, after centuries of plunder, the Third World is owed money. In this case, they suggest, the financial debt should be exchanged for the "eco-debt." Calculations of the environmental damage done by the private sector and rich nations, such as climate change or the destruction of rain forests, measured against the environmental benefits contributed by the people and lands of the developing world, such as providing the raw materials of valuable medicines and absorbing excess carbon in those remaining forests, invariably reverse the creditor-debtor relationship.

Foreign aid is another top priority for providing immediate help to the needy. Of the world's fifty poorest countries, this type of "overseas development assistance," or ODA, as it is called, made up more than four out of every five dollars flowing into their economies—while they got less than one out of every twenty dollars of private foreign investment worldwide. For decades, the UN has encouraged richer countries to meet agreed commitments to contribute at least 0.7 percent of their gross domestic product toward foreign aid, but just six countries—Norway, Denmark, the Netherlands, Sweden, Finland, and Luxembourg—have consistently met this pledge. Of its massive gross domestic product—a total of about $10 trillion in goods and services produced in 2002—the United States provides as little as 0.1 percent. The average contribution by all the industrialized countries is just 0.22 percent.

Together, all the industrialized nations provide $50 billion in overseas development assistance, just half of what analysts suggest is needed to meet the goal of cutting poverty in half by the year 2015. This goal, along with numerous other quantifiable targets for improving worldwide welfare, has been reaffirmed over and over— most recently in the UN Millennium Declaration of 2000, the WTO Doha Declaration of 2001, and at two 2002 conferences: the Monterrey Consensus on Financing for Development and the Johannesburg World Summit on Sustainable Development. In Monterrey, President Bush announced the United States would increase its annual contribution to ODA by $5 billion starting in 2004 for three years, with a possible continuation through 2010—but only for those countries meeting certain conditions, a type of unilateral structural adjustment program.

While famine and other crises call for emergency relief, many civil society groups point out that cash assistance and food aid should be considered short-term remedies that, in the medium-to-long term, can become counter-productive. All too often, aid programs wipe out the productive capacity of the recipients and are tied to conditionalities such as requiring the food, equipment and services be purchased from companies based in the donor countries—stimulating an exodus of the vitally needed cash back to where it started. Some activists propose eliminating bilateral aid altogether, in favor of a single pool of funds to be distributed by a council of representatives of the recipient countries. Another approach is called "triangulated" aid, by which donors could offer their cash contributions to a third party in the same region as the recipient, who would then deliver the food, seeds, construction materials or other relief, thus eliminating the problem with conditions and simultaneously supporting regional economic development.

Priorities for poor countries dependent upon agriculture include regenerating rural productive capacity, starting with free access to locally adapted seeds, and adding to the value of harvests with local processing and sale of finished goods—all off which will require several changes in current trade rules. Small- and medium-size enterprises could be supported with linkages to manufacturing and other industrial sectors in the region, achieving economies of scale that, with government backing and reasonable financing, might withstand foreign competition—especially if prohibitions on dumping were enforced. Low interest rates, targeted tax breaks and incentives, tariffs protective of basic industries, limits on speculative financial flows, fair employment policies and investments in public health, education and infrastructure are all government-driven mechanisms that develop productive jobs and long-term economic capacity. This combination, government intervention to support local resource development alongside a targeted industrial strategy, is necessary to regenerate national and regional economies that benefit the poor.

As a first step to enable these priorities, rather than the prevailing approach, substantial debt relief and unconditional terms (or at least very different conditions!) on new loans and additional aid and investment resources are urgently needed. Poor countries must be allowed to exercise their sovereignty in directing these resources towards the most strategic social and economic goals, which will also require a reversal of current international-policy trends. Consultative, participatory and other democratic processes are necessary to ensure wise decisionmaking but they also engage the public and the poor in implementing local development strategies.

Like-minded and like-resourced nations can construct regional agreements that defend their economies from predatory trade and speculative investment behavior, and from economic contagion spilling over from financial instability elsewhere in the global system. At the same time, the international community and the leaders of the richer countries must take responsibility for stabilizing the global financial system and redirecting capital flows strategically to invest in equitable development throughout the world.

Along these lines, the billionaire financier George Soros has proposed that the IMF issue a new allocation of its special currency, SDRs, toward providing public services in developing countries. If successful, it could be repeated regularly. The Soros proposal stipulates that all IMF members with larger foreign-exchange reserves, including relatively well-off countries like China and Botswana, agree in advance to donate their share of the new allocation to ODA. There is a precedent of sorts. In 1997, the IMF members agreed to amend the Articles of Incorporation to allow a single special "equity" issue of SDRs to channel funds—about $28 billion—to the former Soviet republics and other poorer countries. But it still needs to be approved by an 85 percent majority of the IMF vote, and since the U.S. Congress has refused to ratify the deal, withholding our 17.5 percent decisive share of the vote.

Soros's proposal also stipulates a new governance mechanism for this fund that reflects Keynes's call for decision making by professionals independent of their governments. This independent board would not have authority for disbursing the money; instead, it would be charged with devising an annual strategy and a menu of options for projects from which the donors of the SDRs would be free to choose. Actual distribution of the funds would take place directly at the community level via a single lead development agency such as the UN Development Program. All in all, Soros's proposal amounts to a shift of financial resources from rich to poor, creating a significant fund for development in the Third World.

Another funding mechanism could be based on the model of the Multilateral Fund mandated by the Montreal Protocol on ozone depletion. The Montreal Protocol's fund is financed by industrialized countries through donations assessed according to their level of mandatory contributions to the UN. The fund's governance structure ensures equity amongst industrialized and developing countries by giving each bloc seven representatives and requiring that all decisions enjoy a majority vote of both blocs. Its resources are devoted to helping developing countries avoid and phase out ozone-depleting chemicals, but this model could be replicated in other technology transfer and development programs.

There is also a proposal on the table at the UN Food and Agriculture Organization to support a global fund derived from a tax on all royalties paid for patents and other intellectual property rights on plants. This fund would allocate revenues to farmer-led programs for the diversification of plant genetic resources for food and agriculture.

Indeed, there are numerous possibilities for taxing internationally traded products, particularly those that generate great wealth for a few companies, and having revenues then redistributed by some type of global taxing authority: one that is transparent, democratic, and mandated to ensure equitable investment toward poverty alleviation and sustainable development throughout the world.

3. The Public Interest and Human Rights

Markets are for buying and selling. Those with little or no purchasing power are left out. Even well-managed markets cannot provide what the poor need, or the intangible stuff (air and dignity, justice and peace) that cannot be bought and sold. Another part of the definition of "public goods"—as these socially valuable, hard-to-market things are called—is the notion that they can be shared universally: my having air, dignity, justice, and peace does not deprive you from having them too. But times change. Until recently, people tended to include water on this list! The water companies have certainly figured out how to buy and sell water, and people in deserts know how little they can depend upon universal sharing.

Public services have evolved as society's way of providing some public goods to the whole community. Where markets fail to provide public goods and services, civil society has often empowered their governments to create laws and institutions that will. The governments unite their taxpayers' purchasing power to provide water and sanitation systems, health and education, public parks, police and fire protection, cultural events, pollution prevention, and so on. While a lot of rich individuals do buy their own purified water, private parkland, personal security, private tutors, and personal physicians in the marketplace, it is probably not possible for every human being to do so.

However, if all 497 billionaires on Earth (as counted by *Forbes* in 2002) donated $1 billion each to one of the global funds, the resulting jackpot of $497 billion would go a long way; that is, if the fund were governed transparently enough to be incorruptible, and democratically enough to be spent equitably. Why, $100 billion is all it would take to meet the Millennium Declaration goal of cutting poverty in half by 2015. Even so, this model is based on charity rather than self-sufficiency. Holding corporations to account for their appropriations of labor and the environment would go a longer way toward sustainable development and peace. However, progressive members of civil society aren't the only ones at work to take the edge off the market's ruthlessness. Corporate lobbies garner great subsidies, their own form of welfare, in the bailouts of private enterprise.

There is a labor market, of course. But labor markets, like most markets, suffer from "market failures"—that is, factors that interfere with the so-called free exchange between equally endowed buyers and sellers. Over and over again, action on the part of governments has been necessary to establish and protect the rights of workers. In the United States, as in other countries, plenty of trade unionists have lost their lives in efforts to win national legislation guaranteeing their right to organize and bargain collectively, to the eight-hour day, the five-day week, and so forth. The same is true in lots of other countries. Unfortunately, the IMF and World Bank have deliberately used structural adjustment to drive down wage rates, and transnational corporations freely relocate their operations to lower-wage countries where labor rights are not well protected, leaving thousands of unemployed behind in destitute communities. Many companies deliberately employ illegal immigrants at illegally low wages under inhumane, sometimes toxic conditions, aware they cannot file complaints. Some even contract with smugglers, who bring in shipments of workers under conditions of virtual slavery. And in the growing sex markets workers are likewise treated as slaves.

There is also a market for culture—theater and dance

tickets at twenty-five dollars a pop, eco-tourism visits to exotic villages in the Himalayas, pre-Columbian artifacts and contemporary handicrafts all sell well—but this market does not provide cultural security in the least. To the contrary, the merchandising of traditional communities often destroys their way of life, bringing them ever closer to actual demise. Eco-tourism can bring much-needed revenue to remote communities, but it can also convert their daily routine into performance and create dependency. Indigenous art is frequently pirated for sale in the marketplace and display in museums, or merely to inspire commercial designs. Anthropologists employed by pharmaceutical companies pirate indigenous knowledge in their search for medicinal plants. Dams, agricultural "modernization," and other so-called development projects continue to displace millions of indigenous peoples from their homes. Some six hundred languages, and the communities that speak them, have become extinct in the past century, and another three thousand are considered in danger of extinction in the next few decades.

With an eye to moving all nations towards meeting basic human needs and protecting basic human rights, the UN Universal Declaration of Human Rights (UDHR) of 1948 lays out very specific entitlements due all people on Earth. "Everyone has the right to a standard of living adequate for the health and well-being of himself and of his family, including food, clothing, housing and medical care and necessary social services," it states. "Everyone has the right to work, to free choice of employment, to just and favorable conditions of work and to protection against unemployment" as well as "just and favorable remuneration" and the "right to form and to join trade unions." In addition, everyone has "the right freely to participate in the cultural life of the community, to enjoy the arts and to share in scientific advancement and its benefits." Among dozens of other rights, the UDHR adds that everyone is entitled to a "social and international order in which the rights and freedoms set forth in this Declaration can be fully realized."

Two subsequent treaties, called covenants, define more specifically the obligations of national governments to ensure these rights: the Covenant on Civil and Political Rights and the Covenant on Economic, Social, and Cultural Rights. Each is managed by a UN committee that reviews the behavior of the participating governments and makes recommendations for changes in their national policies and practices to fulfill the obligations. Recently, the Committee on Economic, Social, and Cultural Rights has begun a "dialogue" with the World Bank, IMF, and WTO examining how their policies have affected the capacity of nation-states to protect and promote these human rights.

The ILO has established 184 conventions to protect and promote labor rights. ILO Convention 169 eloquently addresses the rights of indigenous peoples, as do the Convention on Biological Diversity and the Draft Declaration on the Rights of Indigenous Peoples—a UN text prepared in consultation with representatives of the First Nations themselves, which now awaits ratification and implementation by the official UN governments.

These rights include, first and foremost, the right to self-determination. They also include the rights of people to manage their own lands and natural resources, legal and economic systems, science, technology, art, and culture.

While human rights, defined broadly, have been well articulated in the UN's extensive legal system, advocates today must focus on developing effective enforcement mechanisms, [See appendix]—although this is one of those things that is much easier said than done. Under existing international law, each sovereign state has the option to commit itself to each particular treaty. For example, only sixty-nine countries have ratified all of the fundamental conventions of the ILO, and the United States has ratified only two of them—keeping company with China, Burma, Oman, and Armenia in this dubious distinction.

While urging enforcement of international law, however, pro–global justice activists most certainly do not seek uniformity on a global scale—quite the contrary! But as long as economic and political pressures can force countries to accept the WTO's jurisdiction over their own economies' in the interests of commercial enterprise, a coordinated economic and political strategy must be devised amongst the rest of the world to force the United States and other international "outlaws" to accept minimal standards for labor rights, environmental and ecosystem protection, indigenous peoples' cultural sovereignty, and other human rights recognized by the community of nations.

Proposals for strengthening international enforcement mechanisms include more frequent use of joint economic sanctions, such as those exercised against South Africa and Iraq. Another proposal would link UN agreements with WTO rules to invoke the WTO's powerful dispute settlement system against violators of the UN rules. But to implement such proposals fairly, and ensure truly social objectives, requires developing a broad-based multilateral mandate in democratic consultation with civil society. This is precisely what spawned sanctions against the apartheid government in South Africa and facilitated that country's transition to democracy. This type of consensus-building did not precede the violent war against Iraq, nor the imposition of sanctions against Iraq for years before that, and the failure to do so now haunts not just the long-suffering Iraqi people but the whole world.

Other proposals suggest creating new multilateral institutions with mandates that, similar to the WTO itself or the conditionalities of the World Bank and IMF, take authority over national governments. Only in this case they would not prioritize commercial and financial returns, but oblige conformance with international social and environmental policy. Another option would involve empowering the International Court of Justice or the Permanent Court of Arbitration to settle conflicts between international agreements.

Governmental action can also intervene to correct market failures in another way, without creating new institutions or new international authority. For example, the tools of public policy can be used to create economic incentives and disincentives that stimulate "market-based" behavior toward social goals. Flip-flopping the concept of public goods, proponents of such "market mechanisms" argue that taxes, subsidies, tolls, tradable permits, and other mechanisms "internalize" the costs or, in other words, eliminate the profitability of "bad" behavior such as the dumping of wastes. These economic policies, while still dependent upon government action, can shift patterns of production and generate resources for alternative investments.

Some proposals for "market-based" cost internalization mechanisms involve:

➤ taxes on carbon, nitrogen, gasoline, kerosene, and other fossil fuels;

➤ tolls on the long-distance transport of goods that accrue in a fund for investing in renewable energy;

➤ trading schemes that permit certain levels of pollution and auction off the surpluses, limiting total emissions;

➤ the elimination of subsidies that encourage trade in scarce or harmful products alongside the creation of new subsidies, perhaps through public bond issues, to provide low-cost, long-term financing to develop more benign forms of production;

➤ third-party certification and the labeling of products so willing buyers may choose more benign products;

- customs tariffs that charge exporting companies for the costs of handling waste disposal and cleanup in the importing country; and

- liability provisions that make manufacturers responsible for the costs of handling damage and cleanups, as well as parallel bonding requirements for up-front insurance.

Another proposal for cost internalization has been dubbed "full-cost accounting." Historically, natural resources have been undervalued; only as they become scarce does society appreciate their full value, which may even exceed commercial prices set in a market. For example, in addition to providing shelter, firewood, and habitat for millions of species of creatures, forests are now understood to retain water and prevent flooding. They also sequester carbon in woody tissue and slow global warming. These "ecological services" are valuable to the public, even if they are not reflected in the price of wood.

Economists nowadays are proposing that the way economic growth is measured could be adapted to more fully account for real costs. Thus, the depletion of natural resources, including timber, oil, minerals, and fish, might more accurately be counted as a net loss of a nation's assets, rather than as net growth in gross domestic product through their commercial sale. Government officials seeing this type of balance sheet might decide that spending a particular asset faster than it can be reproduced actually jeopardizes their country's economy. So, too, the

World Bank and IMF might want to alter their structural adjustment policies to reflect this understanding, in order to protect their debtors' assets over the long term, ensuring their future productivity and sustainable development. But caution is called for. Especially for developing countries in negotiations over aid or structural adjustment packages, the premature application of these accounts could become prejudicial. Comparisons between countries are particularly inappropriate—at least until a standardized methodology has been widely tested and found to be fair by all.

A good place to start might be the energy sector: developing a reasonable mechanism to internalize the full costs of its extraction, refinement, transport, varied uses, relative emissions, and waste disposal from cradle to grave. All too often, the hidden costs tend to accrue on one side of a trade deal while the clear financial benefits accrue on the other—like when oil spills destroy entire villages in Nigeria or Colombia or the Arctic yet the oil companies still profit as U.S. consumers keep flooring their SUVs. In the international context, this kind of analysis should be sure to identify the full costs from "cradle-to-export-border and from import-border-to-grave," as one report from the UN Conference on Trade and Development proposed.

Public policies are needed to establish and enforce the provision of public services, and the protection of public goods, from the community level to the international level. Public education is essential to increase our awareness of the global implications of our individual and national behavior, so that our collective sense of responsibility generates the political will to comply with the UDHR. Individuals, communities, nations, corporations, the WTO and World Bank and IMF, and all the other institutions of our society should be held accountable to the UDHR and all the other social and environmental treaties—thus constructing a "social and international order in which the rights and freedoms set forth in this Declaration can be fully realized." It might even look like democracy and justice.

4. Corporate Regulation

When Eastern Europe opened its borders to capitalism, the UN sponsored a survey of four hundred corporate executives asking about their strategies for locating new subsidiaries. Labor costs were nearly always their first consideration, but taxation and transfer pricing (manipulating prices on transactions between subsidiaries of the same firm) were near the top of their lists. Several companies acknowledged they keep two sets of books, one for the tax authorities and one for themselves. Post-Enron, we've become aware that many such accounting practices are not even illegal—and that corporate corruption is fairly widespread.

Dozens of sets of voluntary guidelines for responsible business practices exist—some established by the businesses themselves, such as the Responsible Care program of the chemical industry; some by the UN, including the Global Compact; and others by intergovernmental agencies such as the World Bank and the Organization for

Economic Cooperation and Development. Both corporate and civil society leaders are cooperating in a Coalition for Environmentally Responsible Economies (CERES) to develop a standard for corporate disclosure of environmental management and labor practices called the Global Reporting Initiative. All of these contribute to shedding light on corporate behavior and encouraging greater public accountability, but there is very little obligation.

Labor and student activists have successfully highlighted the unfair labor practices of many corporations, including Nike and The Gap, that have utilized child labor in sweatshop conditions and otherwise abused workers' rights. These successful campaigns, relying on a lot of highly visible negative publicity, have induced many companies to clean up their operations in the places that were highlighted. Unfortunately, the companies have not reformed their labor practices everywhere they do business, and in some cases, after the television cameras go home and public pressure eases, it's back to business –as usual. The activists continue their monitoring and publicity, but it's simply not possible to effectively do so on a worldwide basis.

Virtually every national government has some degree of regulatory authority over companies doing business within its territory; but as companies went global there was no parallel process for globalizing governance of their behavior. A comprehensive approach for building an international regime for corporate regulation might start with expanding the use of national law, then emphasizing regional capacity and institution-building, and finally constructing links among the regions until a global system is in place.

At the national level, activists could work for legislation to hold parent companies accountable for all their subsidiaries everywhere they do business. This could include global compliance with the home country's labor, safety, health, and environmental regulations, and require the publication of records on financial solvency, liabilities, employment decisions, health and safety, and so on by all subsidiaries of the parent companies. The publication of payments for mining concessions (which often amount to a form of veiled bribery) and offshore tax havens, too, could be regulated through national legislation. While much easier said than done, simultaneous campaigns in numerous countries targeting the same transnational company could convince its management to raise standards across the corporate chain.

At the regional level, data-sharing systems on nationally held business information such as taxes paid, number of employees, trade volumes by product categories, injuries and accidents, and environmental compliance might help build the capacity to set common regional standards. Regional registration of companies of a certain size—setting thresholds for number of employees, number of national affiliates, total assets in the region, or regional sales volumes—could avoid duplicative record keeping in neighboring countries too. Perhaps regional agreements could be reached for common requirements amongst the parallel national agencies—labor relations, health departments, food safety and environmental protection agencies, securities and accounting regulatory authorities, and so on—so that companies could not evade such standards simply by moving their business to another country. Or maybe regional agreements could mandate that the most stringent labor, safety, health, and environmental regulations of any country in the region be applicable throughout the region. Regional antitrust policies to break up monopolistic firms could be based on the best national laws of the United States, United Kingdom, Germany, and Japan. Why not set up a regional taxing authority, regional liability obligations, and a regional enforcement mechanism, using the national courts?

Strong regional capacity might form the best foundation for constructing a global system of corporate regulation. This, too, might begin by establishing links among all regional offices, sharing information and building an ever- greater common data base; obligating every transnational corporation to adhere to the most stringent labor, safety, health, and environmental regulations of any country where it operates; and designing globally enforceable civil and criminal sanctions. Eventually, the community of nations might be ready to hold transnational corporations reaching a certain threshold of size accountable to the conventions of the ILO, international human rights agreements, and the multilateral environmental agreements.

As with the management of public goods and services, accounting mechanisms to internalize social and environmental factors may be a first step to foster more responsible business practices. "Triple bottom-line accounting," for example, proposes corporate reports publish three sets of indicators: one measuring the financial bottom line, one measuring the bottom line for employee health and welfare, and one measuring environmental performance. However, some degree of government action is probably necessary to ensure the consistency and thus the reliability and fairness of such tools. If some companies report wastewater recycling and paternal-leave policies while their competitors announce wastewater treatment before discharge and an extended disability program, potential investors and customers may have difficulty comparing the available information.

The Global Reporting Initiative (GRI) is an alliance of environmentalists, socially responsible investors, and professional accountants who together are trying to standardize how this type of data gets reported. Companies following the GRI's voluntary guidelines must provide data on their environmental practices, compensation, diversity, community investment, and philanthropic commitments. The Corporate Sunshine Working Group is lobbying the U.S. Securities and Exchange Commission to make the GRI guidelines mandatory.

Other "indicators" have been devised to evaluate corporate performance in different areas. A group known as Transparency International has developed a set of indicators to measure corruption. Nongovernmental organizations working with the UN Food and Agriculture Organization are developing indicators for sustainable agricultural production. Indigenous peoples propose a set of cultural indicators to be reflected in corporate reports. Any of these factors could be built into a model that is applied to screen and evaluate corporate bids for World Bank and other public projects, corporate bids for procurement contracts with public agencies, and the corporate beneficiaries of export credit agencies.

Comparisons of corporate reports across national and cultural borders must be handled with great care, however; sustainable production methods in some ecosystems would be quite unsustainable in others. Purely on the financial side, standardization is not nearly adequate for international comparisons as yet. When Germany's Daimler-Benz corporation decided to list itself on the New York Stock Exchange, the Securities and Exchange Commission required a uniform listing of its assets throughout its group of companies—and the result increased its bottom-line value by some 4 billion deutsche marks!

The UN's Transnational Corporations and Management Division has been working to develop a model for "accounting for sustainable development" internationally, as has the International Chamber of Commerce, the Institute of Chartered Accountants in England and Wales, and many others. Eventually, an accepted system evaluating each transnational company's social and environmental responsibility, as well as their general financial health, indexed by an official ratings agency (along the lines of the Dow Jones Sustainability Index) may be achieved.

Marjorie Kelly, publisher of *Business Ethics* magazine,

suggests a very different revision of the bottom line. She points out that the goal of maximizing shareholders' returns is simply a culturally agreed upon bias in business management, and society could instead decide that maximizing employee welfare is the priority. Some simple changes in the structure of corporate accounts would facilitate this shift. Instead of designating gains to employees (payroll) as expenses and gains to shareholders as income, the equation could be reversed. The new goal would be to drive the company's capital income down as low as possible, with gains distributed toward costs, growth, and wage increases. Capital income would still be a necessary cost of doing business, but it could remain relatively fixed. Thus, the business could thrive and the employees would get rich.

Fortunately, the cascade of scandals—Enron, WorldCom, Tyco, Adelphia, Global Crossing, ImClone, and more—has exposed large gaps in corporate regulation. We can hope this will lead to even more deliberate efforts to create standardized systems of accounting across borders, and tighter regulations on the use of derivatives and other financial instruments. So, too, we can hope that the Enron bust will provoke stronger rules governing the relationship between business executives and public officials—not only in the United States but worldwide. Perhaps it is time to reverse the "free trade" concept of investors' rights and instead create new accounting and legal vehicles enshrined in international law that enable citizens to document and sue corporations for financial, social, and environmental abuses in the courts of their home or host country, whichever seem most public-spirited.

5. Democratic Justice and Institutional Reform

Strong democratic institutions are needed at all levels to regulate corporations, protect public and human rights, eliminate poverty, and manage markets—all components of a just and sustainable model of development. Democracy is essential, but justice requires more than democracy: an appreciation of diversity, respect for minorities, and the inclusion of all in the undertaking of civil society.

Thus, a hierarchy of representative authority, vertically integrated from the local to global levels, is not good enough. We must develop stronger horizontal institutions across each of these jurisdictions: regional and hemispheric and global associations of local communities, regional and hemispheric and global associations of parliamentarians, hemispheric and global associations of regional authorities, and so on. The same is true of nongovernmental entities. We must encourage regional, hemispheric, and global associations of small business associations, librarians, housing developers, students, food safety inspectors, nurses and epidemiologists, gardeners, and so on. The resulting social fabric, with tight horizontal woofs and vertical warps, will indeed be strong.

Many of these institutions already exist, some better organized than others. Trade unions, farm groups, and consumer organizations, for example, have local, national, regional, and international structures in place. The

European Parliament is a relatively recent institution with actual governmental authority helping to democratize European relations; it needs a sister regional parliament in the Western Hemisphere and other relatives in Asia and Africa. There is the International Union of Local Authorities (IULA), which gathers hundreds of the world's mayors regularly—not for decision making but for consultation, debate, and recommendation. Similarly, Global Legislators Organization for a Balanced Environment (GLOBE) brings together some eight hundred parliamentarians from more than a hundred countries to consider policy options for sustainable development and bring recommendations home to their national governments. There may be a place for representatives of local, national, and regional authorities to formally advise and perhaps eventually participate in the formal decision making in certain international matters.

The challenge is to create an integrated system that allocates decision making at the most appropriate level. Lord Keynes, one of the founders of the World Bank and IMF, put it this way: "Ideas, knowledge, art, hospitality, travel—these are the things which should of their nature be international. But let goods be homespun whenever it is responsibly and conveniently possible, and above all, let finance be primarily national." In Europe, the term "subsidiarity" has been used to describe a process of shared decision making amongst the nations, regions, and the EU as a whole. The nations have retained their authority over most internal matters, while giving up their sovereignty to the Brussels-based European Commission over currency and foreign affairs, and creating new powers for underrepresented peoples, such as the Basque, through the regionally structured European Parliament.

Ultimately, a hierarchy of decision making could evolve that is explicitly designed to be inclusive of local communities while seeking a broader public-interest agenda across the planet. The emphasis should be on integrated decentralization, not the creation of a unitary globalized government. Regional associations within nations might serve as a sort of transmission belt from the communities to the national capitals, and various regional associations amongst neighboring nations—if they are relieved of the pressure to deregulate their economies through the "free trade" variety of regional negotiations now proliferating—could serve as the transmission belt to global institutions.

The Southern African Development Community (SADC), for example, has developed jointly funded programs for collaboration between its member countries. In one program, these national governments offer support and legal recognition to local communities, nongovernmental organizations, and the private sector to aid in managing forests, wildlife, and protected areas. These African nations were also strong proponents of the international treaty known as the Convention to Combat Desertification. While severely underfunded, this treaty emphasizes the important role of traditional communities and opens the door for the participation of all stakeholders in implementing its mandates through locally accountable national and regional planning processes.

This model, regional planning for global policies to be implemented locally, deserves to be practiced more often. If, let's say, the ministers of agriculture or the ministers of health from Central America met regularly to prepare their proposals for a Latin American development program, it seems likely they would come up with investment strategies quite different from the $3 billion highway program known as Plan Puebla Panama that is being promoted by their presidents. The ongoing negotiation of the proposed FTAA might also benefit from such regional consultations amongst ministers and stakeholders from agriculture, health, and other affected sections, too, and not leave it all to the trade ministers.

Of course, all of the international planning and negotiating processes should seek recommendations from civil society groups—farmers and nurses, trade unions, environmental and other nongovernmental organizations, small- and medium-sized businesses, and yes, even transnational corporations. But why not require their input? Much the way public hearings are mandatory for many local development projects in the United States, formalized mechanisms inviting public review of all the globally inspired projects—including trade negotiations, World Bank investments, structural adjustment programs, aid packages, and UN treaties—could be required. Local planning and oversight mechanisms should also be set up in the districts where the impacts from globally financed projects will occur. While powerful and corrupt decision makers may ignore citizens' recommendations, such processes obligate the disclosure of corporate and governmental plans and related details that, in turn, enable activists and organizers to build awareness, popular support, and political influence.

Another way to engage the public more directly in international processes would be through the creation of global parliaments. Some advocates have proposed a World Parliament with elected regional representatives to provide input to the UN, World Bank, IMF, and WTO. Another proposal would create a directly elected Water Parliament with authority governing all aspects of managing freshwater supplies. This proposal outlines a Water Parliament declaration that access to clean drinking water is a fundamental human right and suggests a pricing policy that reflects this entitlement. Quantities sufficient to meet a household's daily need should be provided free of charge. Enough to supply basic community needs, including subsistence agriculture and sanitation, would be priced at cost. The users of larger amounts would be billed at steeply escalating rates with exorbitant levels considered illegal. It would be up to the Water Parliament to design a system for enforcing this plan, with parliamentary assemblies gathering regularly at the regional level for each of some 215 interstate water basins around the world.

Reform of the existing international institutions is also high on the list of civil society proposals for democratizing global governance. For starters, the governors of the World Bank and IMF ought to take responsibility for weighting the voting rights of countries more fairly—perhaps balancing the shares held by creditors and debtors alike and requiring a majority from each bloc, or allocating shares according to each country's relative population. The WTO should ensure the equal participation of all members in all negotiations, and set up adequate legal and other technical assistance for countries in need. Its dispute settlement system could be multilateralized, so big-economy violators would be sanctioned collectively by all the other members and maybe the smaller-economy violators would be fined according to a reasonable proportion of their gross domestic product, instead of the value of the unfair trade gained; after all, these unfairly acquired funds accrued to companies, not national treasuries. All three of these international institutions should also increase the transparency of their operations, publishing far more of the documents and data informing their decision-making processes than they now do. A time and place for public input could be built into routine procedures.

One particularly insightful set of proposals for international institutional reform has been published in a little report called "Reimagining the Future: Towards Democratic Governance. " In 2000 the Department of Politics at Australia's La Trobe University convened a working group including members of Hawaii's Toda Institute for Global Peace and Policy Research and the Bangkok-based group Focus on the Global South. They came up with a wealth of ideas, including the following specific suggestions for new global governing bodies:

> ➤ a directly elected People's Assembly at the UN, parallel to the General Assembly, to monitor and review its decisions, each elec-

tor having one vote representing about 6 million people;

➤ a Consultative Assembly with representatives recommended by the secretary general and appointed by the General Assembly from the corporate sector, trade union and professional organizations, and the broad nongovernmental public interest sector;

➤ a new UN Department for Disarmament and Arms Regulation with direct links to the secretary-general and the General Assembly;

➤ a regional structure for peacekeeping and humanitarian responses to emergencies, and the preparation of a comprehensive plan for each mission that includes a statement clarifying its legal authority, objectives, impact-assessment process, termination procedures, and a designated peace ombudsperson; and

➤ several new UN institutions including a permanent civilian police force, a Women's Development Bank, a World Educational Fund, a Global Commons Bank, and a Global Knowledge Bank.

The Dag Hammarskjöld Foundation of Sweden published another set of detailed recommendations for democratizing global governance in 1994. Two long-term civil servants at the UN, Erskine Childers and Brian

Urquhart, proposed an extensive reform agenda for the international institutions in their article "Renewing the United Nations System." Their proposals include:

- ➤ creating a directly elected Parliamentary Assembly at the UN, with management oversight and a budget but no voting authority;

- ➤ upgrading the UN office of the high commissioner for human rights to become a UN deputy secretary-general for human rights;

- ➤ consolidating all economic and development functions—not only the multiple agencies and programs of the UN but also those of the WTO, World Bank, and IMF—under one UN development authority, with a deputy secretary-general for development; and

- ➤ converting the Trusteeship Council to a "Council on Diversity, Representation, and Governance," with a mandate to obtain the "widest range of analyses and recommendations on means of peaceably accommodating cultural and ethnic aspirations; providing adequate domestic and international expression to groups hitherto treated as minorities within nation-states but aspiring to such expression; adjusting exogenously established boundaries; and creative options for the transition of societies from traditional centralist nation-state structures."

CONCLUSION

Many thinkers are working on the global governance challenge: If not the status quo, then what? For the governments of Europe and China and India and Brazil it is about their growing power and place in international decision-making institutions. For much of civil society it is about getting rid of the unjust forces that exercise so much power in their daily lives. For pro–global justice campaigners, it's a matter of building new processes of international decision making from the bottom up.

Taking all of this into account, it seems there must be at least four dimensions to the process of reorganizing our international system. First, the process will need to facilitate debates with civil society at the community level all over the world—before, during, and after institutional transformation. Second, it will need to convince the managers of existing institutions to immediately self-correct within the existing framework. Third, it will need to design democratic mechanisms of coherence between and amongst the institutions of society at every level. And fourth, it will need to create new global mechanisms for creating, managing, and redistributing transnational wealth that are just and democratic, reaching local communities.

The democratization of global governance is generating a lot of debate lately—accelerated in no small part by the terrorist attacks of September 11, 2002, and the subsequent threat of extended war. AIDS and other infectious diseases continue to kill millions, while global warming expands the range of the West Nile mosquito and other vectors. Mad cow disease, *E. coli* contamination, and genetically engineered DNA threaten our food supply. Famine, drought, and floods are rampant. A sense of urgency provokes us all.

Momentum is building. Even prominent political leaders are proposing specific and novel mechanisms for redistributing power and wealth:

➤ France's former prime minister Lionel Jospin, for example, called for an Economic and Social Security Council parallel to the UN's existing military-oriented Security Council, as well as taxes on weapons and carbon dioxide, and the creation of a World Environment Organization.

➤ Brazil's new President Luis Ignacio "Lula" da Silva, better known as just "Lula," has announced that the elimination of hunger will be the hallmark of his first administration—starting with cash payments of $14 per family in the poorest part of the country, then creating adequate channels for food distribution to the tens of millions of Brazilians who are now deprived, next reorganizing Brazil's agricultural programs and policy, and finally proposing a regional parliament in southern South America and restructuring the FTAA negotiations to ensure not just economic but social development throughout the Americas.

➤ Gus Speth, former head of the UN development program and now dean of the Yale School of Forestry and Environmental Studies, supports "social and political empowerment of the poor," endorsing an electronically controlled voluntary self-taxing mechanism so millions of individual citizens worldwide can also contribute through tiny surcharges on their daily electronic transactions.

➤ Anthony Hill, former Jamaican ambassador to the WTO, emphasizes the need for "local decision making at local levels," with national as well as international programs giving "absolute priority" to local analysis and local implementation of policies "to provide for decent living conditions."

For some local activists, the basic principle for just and democratic global governance is, to quote my friend from the Philippines: "Leave us alone." For others, like my friend from Bangladesh, it is about communities engaged in cultural resistance—defending their language and dress and cuisine and art and heritage and health and happiness from the onslaught of globalization. As my Ethiopian friend says, it is a matter of sustaining the relationship between human beings and the land, without corporate intermediaries. A couple of friends from Colombia and Uruguay told me: "Don't spend any more time reacting to *their* agenda. We have to create our own." And right here, my friend, my neighbor, where I live on the East Side of St. Paul, says, "Let's take care of our own government first."

"Localization" is not a philosophy of isolationism, but of integrated decentralization in which strong local institutions form the base, with national and regional and international institutions—governmental as well as nongovernmental—networking across the hemispheres, horizontally, as well as from local to global, vertically. National governments remain the point of responsibility and accountability to their citizens. Regional associations serve as the transmission belts of information, planning, and policy making—within nations as well as across national boundaries. Global institutions and decisions must derive their authority from an effective system of communications amongst stakeholders. There is no intention of turning back the clock or restricting the flow of information, trade, and finance. To the contrary, these resources are absolutely essential to restructure production and distribution in ways that are sustainable and promote new models for human development and peace.

What we're talking about is *global democracy*. There is no doubt that people, communities, civil society, the public, whatever you want to call us—*we, the people*—reject the military coercion and market fundamentalism that now dominate the world. We want a just international system that gives undeniable preference to public goods, and investment that promotes food security, sustainable livelihoods, cultural integrity, and human and ecological health. We must insist that our national governments embrace these policies, which in turn will facilitate the development of strong communities with locally embedded social responsibilities and the capacity to share and care globally.

SOURCES

Aga Khan, Sadruddin. *Policing the Global Economy: Why, How and for Whom?* London: Bellerive Foundation, 1998.

Akyuez, Yilmaz. *The Debate on the International Financial Architecture: Reforming the Reformers.* Penang: Third World Network, 2000.

Anderson, Sarah, Phyllis Bennis, and John Cavanagh. *Coalition of the Willing or Coalition of the Coerced? How the Bush Administration Influences Allies in Its War on Iraq.* Washington, D.C.: Institute for Policy Studies, 2003.

Camilleri, J. A., K. Malhotra, and M. Tehranian. *Reimagining the Future Towards Democratic Governance.* Australia: Arena Printing and Publishing, 2000.

Caplan, Ruth. *In Whose Service?: GATS and the FTAA.* Croton-on-Hudson, N.Y.: Apex Press, 2001.

Charles Leopold Meyer Foundation. *From the WTO's Setback at Seattle...To the Conditions for Global Governance.* Paris: Rongead, 2001.

Childer, Erskine, with Brian Urquhart. "Renewing the United Nations System." *Development Dialogue* 2 (1994):1–215.

Citizen's Network on Essential Services. *The World Bank's Performance in Carrying Out the Agenda for Freshwater Resources*. Tides Center: Takoma Park, 2002.

Cleveland, Harlen. *Birth of a New World: An Open Moment for International Leadership*. San Francisco: Jossey-Bass Publishers, , 1993.

Danaher, Kevin. *Ten Reasons to Abolish the IMF & World Bank*. New York: Seven Stories Press, 2001.

Dawkins, Kristin. *Gene Wars: The Politics of Biotechnology*. New York: Seven Stories Press, 2003.

Earth Dialogues. *Compilation of Roundtable Reports*. Lyon, France: Green Cross International, 2002.

Edwards, Michael, and John Gaventa. *Global Citizen Action*. Boulder, Col.: Lynne Rienner Publishers, Inc., 2001.

Edwards, Michael. *Future Positive: International Co-operation in the 21st Century*. London: Earthscan Publications Ltd., 1999.

Esty, Daniel C., and Maria H. Ivanova. *Global Environmental Governance: Options and Opportunities*. New Haven: Yale School of Forestry and Environmental Studies, 2002.

Foster, John W., with Anita Anand. *Whose World Is It Anyway? Civil Society, the United Nations and the*

Multilateral Future. Ottawa: The United Nations Association in Canada, 1999.

Gleckman, Harris, and Riva Krut. *The Social Benefits of Regulating International Business.* Geneva: United Nations Research Institute for Social Development, 1994.

Harland, Cleveland. *Birth of a New World: An Open Moment for International Leadership.* San Francisco: Jossey-Bass Publishers, 1993.

Heinrich Boell Foundation. *Trade and Environment, the WTO, and MEAs: Facets of a Complex Relationship.* Washington, D.C.: The Heinrich Boell Foundation, 2001.

International Institute for Environment and Development and the Regional and International Networking Group. *Financing for Sustainable Development.* Hertfordshire, England: SMI Distribution Services Ltd., 2002.

International Labor Organization. *Ratifications of the ILO Fundamental Conventions.* Available at: http://webfusion.ilo.org/public/db/standards/norms/appl/appl-ratif8conv.cfm?Lang=EN, 2002.

Keck, Margaret E., and Kathryn Sikkink. *Activists Beyond Borders.* Ithaca, N.Y.: Cornell University Press, 1998.

Kelly, Marjorie. *The Divine Right of Capital: Dethroning the Corporate Aristocracy.* San Francisco: Berrett-Koehler Publishers, Inc., 2001.

Kennickell, Arthur B. *An Examination of Changes in the Distribution of Wealth from 1989 to 1998: Evidence from the Survey of Consumer Finances.* Washington, D.C.: Federal Reserve Board, 2000.

Khagram, Sanjeev, James V. Riker, and Kathryn Sikking. *Restructuring World Politics: Transnational Social Movements, Networks, and Norms.* Minneapolis: University of Minnesota Press, 2002.

Kirshner, Orin. *The Bretton Woods–GATT System: Retrospect and Prospect After Fifty Years.* Armonk, N.Y.: M.E. Sharpe, 1996.

Krebs, A. V. *The Corporate Reapers: The Book of Agribusiness.* Washington, D.C.: Essential Books, 1992.

MacArthur, John R. *The Selling of "Free Trade": NAFTA, Washington, and the Subversion of American Democracy.* New York: Hill and Wang, 2000.

McCully, Patrick. *Silenced Rivers: The Ecology and Politics of Large Dams.* London: Zed Books, 2001.

Montague, Peter. "GMOs: The New Threat to Indigenous People." *Wild Matters*, March 2002, 8–9.

Montreal International Forum. *Civil Society Engaging Multilateral Institutions: At the Crossroads.* Chateauguay, Quebec: McCormick & Associates, 1999.

Montreal International Forum. *Promoting Human Security: Civil Society Influence.* Montreal: Michell Garneau, 2000.

Murphy, Sophia. *United States Dumping on World Agricultural Markets*. Minneapolis: Institute for Agriculture and Trade Policy, 2003.

Ocampo, José. *Rethinking the Development Agenda*. Santiago, Chile: Economic Commission for Latin America and the Caribbean, 2001.

Owens, Jeffrey. *International Co-operation in Taxation*. New York: Organisationfor Economic Cooperation and Development, 2002.

Pak, J., and John S. Zdanowicz. *Trade with the World: an Estimate of 2000 Lost U.S. Federal Income Tax Revenues Due to Over-Invoiced Imports and Under-Invoiced Exports*. Miami: Florida International University, 2001.

Perlas, Ncanor. *Shaping Globalization: Civil Society, Cultural Power and Threefolding*. Philippines: Center for Alternative Development Initiatives and Global Network for Social Threefolding, 2000.

Petrella, Riccardo. *The Water Manifesto: Arguments for a World Water Contract*. London: Zed Books, 2001.

Pettifor, Ann. *Chapter 9/11?: Resolving International Debt Crises*. London: New Economics Foundation, 2002.

Public Citizen. *NAFTA's Bizarre Bazaar: The Deal Making that Bought Congressional Votes on the North American Free Trade Agreement*. Washington, D.C.: Public Citizen, 1993.

Raghavan, Chakravarthi. *Recolonization: GATT, the Uruguay Round and the Third World*. Penang: Third World Network, 1990.

Robins, Dorothy B. *Experiment in Democracy*. New York: The Parkside Press, 1971.

Sampson, Gary P. *The Role of the World Trade Organization in Global Governance*. Japan: United Nations University, 2001.

Schirnding, Y., and C.. Mulholland. *Health and Sustainable Development: Key Health Trends*. Geneva: World Health Organization, 2002.

Shrybman, Steven. *The World Trade Organization: A Citizen's Guide*. Toronto: James Lorimer & Company Ltd., 2001.

Simms, Andrew. *An Environmental War Economy*. London: New Economics Foundation, 2001.

Structural Adjustment Participatory Review International Network (SAPRIN). *The Policy Roots of Economic Crisis and Poverty: A Multi-Country Participatory Assessment of Structural Adjustment*. Washington D.C.: SAPRIN, 2002.

Teitel, Martin, and Hope Shand. *The Ownership of Life: When Patents and Values Clash*. Minneapolis: Institute for Agriculture and Trade Policy, 1997.

Transparency International. *The 2002 Transparency International Corruption Perception Index*. Available at: http://www.infoplease.com/ipa/A0781359.html.

United Nations Conference on Trade And Development. *Trade Agreements, Petroleum and Energy Policies.* New York: United Nations, 2000.

Urquhart, Brian. *Between Sovereignty and Globalisation: Where Does the United Nations Fit In?* Uppsala, Sweden: Dag Hammarskjöld Foundation, 2000.

ABOUT THE AUTHOR

Kristin Dawkins is a senior fellow at the Institute of Agriculture and Trade Policy. She worked for sixteen years in community development and public policy research in Philadelphia, including spending nine years as the executive director of the Philadelphia Jobs in Energy Project.